Armond White's *The Resistance: Ten Years of Pop Culture that Shook the World* won acclaim for advancing cultural criticism in 1996. The *San Francisco Bay Guardian* hailed it as the book of the year. He is currently film critic for *New York Press* and pop music writer for *The Nation* magazine. White's essay on the O.J. Simpson trial, "Eye, the Jury" appeared in the anthology *Birth of a Nation 'hood*, edited by Toni Morrison. His cultural writing has appeared in *The New York Times, The Village Voice, Spin, Film Comment, Sight and Sound* and many others. He was chairman of the New York Film Critics Circle in 1994 and won the ASCAP–Deems Taylor Award for Music Criticism in 1992. His music video presentations, *Change the Style. West of MTV, Romank Fiction, Crossculture Dreams* and *DreamWorlds* have been invited to film and video festivals from New York to Dallas to Tokyo, Japan. A native of Detroit, Michigan, he currently lives in New York City.

Parental Advisory

Rebel for the Hell of It was written before the March 9, 1997 killing of The Notorious B.I.G. I let all comment on that artist stand as proof of the significance he shared with Tupac in representing the picture of hiphop. I also want to remind all those hiphop exploiters who claimed the rationale behind the 1992 Los Angeles uprising was already in the music to keep rap in the perspective it deserves. Pious moralizing about the violent deaths of Tupac and Biggie Smalls suggests that many people still don't take the music seriously. Had they really comprehended hiphop, they would have expected these rappers to die horribly, suddenly, predictably. Tupac and Biggie weren't clairvoyant but they were part of a culture system that dangerously capitalizes on Black talent while undervaluing Black life.

REBEL FOR THE HELL OF IT

The Life of TUPAC SHAKU

An Interpretation by Armond White

Quartet Books

First published in Great Britain by Quartet Books Limited
A member of the Namara Group
27 Goodge Street
London W1P 2LD

A catalogue record for this book is available from the British Library

ISBN 0 7043 8049 8

Printed and bound in Great Britain by C. P. D. Wales Ltd

Contents

Introduction

Tears twinkled like stars in Afeni Shakur's eyes as she told a TV interviewer of hearing about the death struggle of her son, Tupac Shakur: 'The doctor came out and said that Tupac had stopped breathing. Three times. And they had revived him three times. And that every time they revived him he just went back. And I asked them to leave him alone and to let him go. I really felt it was important for Tupac, who fought so hard to have a free spirit. I thought it was important for his spirit to be allowed to be free. And so I rejoiced with him and the release of his spirit. I rejoiced then, and I rejoice now when I'm not crying.'

Afeni did not cry alone. Hiphop followers around the world mourned the death of one of pop music's most charismatic stars. Tupac's first two albums, *2pacalypse Now* and *Strictly for My N.I.G.G.A.Z.*, sold enough copies for each to qualify for gold record status; his third, *Me Against the World*, reached that level within its first year of release; and his subsequent albums all went straight to the Number One chart position, with the posthumus Makaveli album, *The Don Killuminati the Seven-Day Theory*, selling over 600,000 copies in its first week. These statistics prove an eager, committed audience – a sign of fan devotion that in itself signifies Tupac's importance in pop music and in the hearts of those who responded to his art.

Those hearts were broken by two events in the fall of 1996. First, on September 7, when Tupac was shot in Las Vegas. He had just witnessed a heavyweight championship fight of Mike Tyson, a recently jailed pop icon like himself, with whom he had shared ideas on improving their social status. After the fight, Tupac rode in a black BMW 750 with Marion 'Suge' Knight, his new mentor and owner of Death Row Records, heading for Knight's Vegas Club 662 to celebrate Tyson's victory as their own (on the way out of the fight Tupac and Knight scuffled with another vagrant crew). On Flamingo Road, their caravan of six cars stopped at a red light. A white Cadillac pulled up alongside and a man got out of it, walked over to Tupac's window seat and shot him. Tupac took four bullets – he wasn't wearing his usual protective bulletproof vest – and Knight was grazed. Ambulances rushed Tupac to the University Medical Center.

Second heartbreak: on September 13 Tupac died as a result of respiratory problems. Doctors had removed one lung to assist his breathing, but internal bleeding continued. He also underwent a medically induced coma. After a week, the rapper's fight ended.

But Tupac's memory plays on with the records he made, chronicling his remarkable story. He was the son of Black activists and a potent force in the most exciting cultural movement of the century's last two decades. For audiences in search of a voice and as a figure expressing their impatience and anger, Tupac created a body of work that spoke from all sides of the times' confusion – the devolution of social ideals in the era of naked, shameless, direct, brutal exploitation. When Tupac's passion left the earth, loving listeners could, like Afeni, rejoice that he no longer suffered the indignity of laboring under hiphop's shrill corporate take-over in the last few years. This development upset his ideals about individual revolution and demanded that listeners and artists alike exchange their deepest feelings for their value in the music industry's marketplace.

Tupac's achievement as a pop artist was based on notions of unruly behavior that would once have seemed revolutionary but now, in an era of compromise, had become as common as everyday frustration and the endless search for joy. The outcome of those ideas was largely embodied by Tupac's own fate, and tragically acted out by his assassination, his disparagement, his death, his suppression – the four bullets fired, as often in modern tragic tales, by a 'brother.'

We lost Tupac before he died. His embodiment of reckless Black defiance delighted hiphop heads while they thrilled to such popular tunes as 'California Love,' 'Keep Your Head Up' and 'Dear Mama,' the imperishable story of a son's love for his mother's strength but mostly for her ideas (it's in the groove). Not much pride or familial concern was voiced over Tupac's self-destructive acts while he lived – only sideline observations and an occasional pat on the head, just like bad parents give. And so Tupac himself bequeathed to the hiphop nation the same irrational bluster that he could depend upon to get attention. Like the late rap impresario Eazy E (Eric Wright), Tupac has left behind complicated legacies of thuggish-ness/caring, seriousness/silliness, affection/crime, sex/violence and, through it all, pride. Tupac's paradoxes stand right next to the defilement mainstream media sponsors for Black people and the celebration of success that many Black folks, following the dictates of the Reagan era, respect as much as personal integrity.

Sentiment swelled for Tupac's death-defying conduct and this well-meant indulgence, in part, prevented him from receiving the good counsel and safe company that might have kept him alive. Thus his reputation and, most importantly, his *effect* grow. This is the crossroads – not the same as Robert Johnson's legendary place of decision but the everyday, common choice Black folks have to make to determine whether to live their lives rigorously or carelessly.

Tupac's death raises questions about the future of Black popular music and the roles that musicians and the music industry play in sustaining a discussion of contemporary social problems and human potential. Not only are these the basic themes in rap music – behind the scenarios of gang wars, drug-selling and sexual competition – but they are also the very issues comprising Shakur's life and art.

Tupac's embrace of the hard stance, the wild movement and behavioral extremes – explained by his various hot justifications – were part of the disintegrating moral center. Young folks, already disillusioned, had begun to slip through the cracks. As old-fashioned social remedies lost their value and appeal, the young also lost their elders' sympathy. A moral impasse resulted.

If such a thing as middle-aged rap artists existed, there might be records that dealt with this new lost-generation phenomenon. The closest pop I can think of is British singer Morrissey's 1992 'The National Front Disco,' with its canny lament: 'Where is our boy? / Oh, we've lost our boy! / But I should know / Where you've gone / Because again and again you've explained.' Tupac's anger fits those lines; the next ones account for his reasons: 'There's a country / You don't live there / But one day you would like to / And then you'll show them what you're made of / Oh, then you might do.'

Like Tupac, Morrissey's controversial song received little sympathetic scrutiny – even in England – because it requires a bold confrontation with the fact of social unrest and the quite human chasing after a desperate, if illogical, sense of purpose. Black American pop fans hardly crossed over to Morrissey's playlist, but ironically they might have been the song's most perceptive audience – not, of course, through the view of fascism but by recognizing the song's primordial, nearly nostalgic faith in political association.

Tupac represented the most alarming characteristics of that song – the dissatisfaction felt by people estranged from the political circumstances they were born into. As a result, unwise, faulty, dangerous choices are made by young people looking for answers but fooled by a pandering, unhelpful social system. Earlier generations might have known how to react, through traditional routes of revolt and protest, but in the past twenty years protest has lost its luster and aspiration has become embarrassing except when for money. 'Cash rules everything around me,' as Wu Tang Clan say in 'C.R.E.A.M.'

Black American youth, probably more so than the British disenfranchised, felt additional weight from the race-based system of oppression and discouragement. By the early nineties, the harm of that system was extensive though increasingly disavowed by the mainstream. Meanwhile, social options for Black youth decreased – even the possibility of effective rebellion. Thus, in both American and British youth cultures, two kinds of youth appeared, the capitalist and the social renegade (which would include a lower-order apostate, the slacker). Neither group was mutually exclusive – they'd been raised believing in the power of the capitalist state – and the music industry made profitable fodder of them all. Our loss of Tupac has much to do with the manner in which an industry could deceive him and his peers by manipulating in such a way as to appease simultaneously their political desperation and their material yearning.

Miscomprehension, another modern epidemic, explains how both Tupac and Morrissey's song could appall people. Jailed activist Sanyika Shakur, writing about Tupac's death, used a superb word, 'overstand,' that gets us close to penetrating such pop-culture alarm. 'Overstand' challenges the ideology we take for granted in the word 'understand' by asserting our command of ideas over the existence of established rules and law. While Tupac and Morrissey represent different, almost contrasting responses to social ills, the difficulties they raise require pop audiences to think for themselves about the personal pain of social distress. Tupac put it succinctly when, on the album *All Eyez on Me*, he worried, 'Will I die if I don't go pop?'

To overstand Tupac's life and career means conquering corporate exploitation as well as the myths of Black consciousness that the rapper himself could never reconcile, perhaps because he thought he *understood* them so well.

As Russell Simmons eulogized in *The Source*, 'Tupac wasn't headed for this anymore than say Sean Penn or Kurt Cobain. It was just that rebelliousness for the sake of it, that wild rock-n-roll side of him, that did this. The attitude in our world, especially in youth culture, promotes all of this.'

This book is an effort to make sense of 'all of this' – Tupac and the context in which he lived. Unsettled by the mass atonement occasioned by that particular drive-by shooting, I mourn for the meanings lost to those people who either follow or distrust Black culture. To overstand this ignorance I have attempted a study of Tupac's art-life (not mutually exclusive). He belonged to a great period in American cultural history and his art-life makes the most sense when viewed through the auspicious moment that is hiphop.

It's easy to say, 'Fuck you!' There's no swifter mechanism for social defense; every person who lives Black in America needs to keep a 'fuck you' in his back pocket. But when that handy phrase doesn't get you what you need, it's time for strategy, which means contemplation. And that's what distinguishes the richest rap songs from the simplest ones. Rebelling for the hell of it means saying 'Fuck you,' but in going from a revolutionary ambition to Thug Life Tupac proved it was never enough. In 1995 he said, 'I'm going to save these young niggas because nobody else wants to save them. Nobody ever came to save me. They just watch what happen to you. That's why Thug Life to me is dead. If it's real, then let somebody else represent it, because I'm tired of it.' And yet, when posing for the cover of

All Eyez on Me, he threw up a 'W' hand sign to taunt East Coast–West Coast rivalry, then claimed, 'It's a W for war!'

If it helps to mend that terrible, unnecessary riff, I have taken *Ready to Die*, the debut album by The Notorious B.I.G., as a model. Deep down, despite his differences with Biggie Smalls, Tupac loved the album, which summed up the hiphop aesthetic. Its insight and wit caught his attention, as it did the attention of everyone who has heard it. And that fascination is correct, a reason to come together if only for reflection. *Ready to Die*'s vision of life is movie-style vivid. The opening cut sets up a hiphop biography. A child's – Biggie's – birth surprises its young parents, whose ecstasy doesn't last long. The sound of labor pains recalls the birth description in Ice Cube's 'The Product': 'I was told / Cuz I didn't witness the whole act / In and out was the movement of the bozack / It hot and sweaty with lots of pushin' / Then the nut came gushin' / And it was hell tryin' to bail to the ovary / With nothin' but the Lord lookin' over me / I was white with a tail / But when I reached the finish line / YOUNG BLACK MALE!'

But Biggie doesn't start off so cynically; there's comforting, resonant Black pop in the background at different stages of the youngster's life:

BIRTH: Curtis Mayfield's 'Superfly'
SCHOOL MISCHIEF/PARENTAL FIGHT: 'Rapper's Delight'
SUBWAY MUGGING: Audio Two's 'Top Billin''
JAIL RELEASE: Snoop's 'Gin and Juice'

Tupac admired the way Biggie kept pace with the historical development of Black pop, showing rappers' engagement with the form and the music's connection to real life. The seventies rock critic's notion of using music as a soundtrack to life is trashed here by a deeper, more interesting analogy that takes the message, the tone, the feel of pop – not as background or foreground but as *expression*. This may be a particular feeling of the hiphop generation, whose modern experience is both defined and substantiated by pop music and the culture surrounding it.

Subsequently, the updating track 'Things Done Changed' beautifully shades nostalgia with a palpable series of harp arpeggios, conveying how pop permeates emotion. Each track on *Ready to Die* can be taken as a piece of the world – a piece of hiphop itself. Turned on to his culture, Biggie becomes a part of it. And that's what this book is intended to do: its implicit narrative confirms that the topics of hiphop records – crime, anger, sex, dope (what, no politics?) – are also the real stuff of rappers' lives (thus politics). Proof comes through the imaginative production, vibrant lyrics and the profane but fully engaged voices of both Tupac and Biggie.

Similarly, Tupac needs to be situated among the records, movies, plays and other cultural events that taught him how to think about the world and how to talk about his place in it. Chapter by chapter, *Rebel for the Hell of It* moves through events in Tupac's art and life, shifting like a CD changer from the ambitions of his adolescence as a drama student in Baltimore to the important story of his parents' political legacy and the music culture that expressed it. Tupac's migration west to northern California is followed by an explanation in 'Chapter Four of his ideological upbringing. Tupac's first album and his first film are detailed; then the self-assessment in relation to his hiphop peers that began with his second album. Chapter Eight examines Tupac's experience as a cultural icon, followed by the souring events in Hollywood during the filming of *Poetic Justice*. Chapter Ten focuses on Tupac's mounting legal hassles, which are next amplified by the answers back he recorded in *Me Against the World*, with Chapter Eleven examining the history and emotions behind his most beloved song, 'Dear Mama,' then his increased reputation in the world of hiphop that led to moral temptation and an infatuation with criminal insolence that brought him to Death Row's door. The final year of Tupac's life begins with Chapter Fifteen's discussion of his two-disc epic *All Eyez on*

Introduction

Me. Next, the double consciousness of Tupac's Makaveli *alter ego* is examined, then his posthumous image in mainstream media, concluding with his efforts to create a permanent hiphop aesthetic on screen and a final consideration of the moral and political stakes he raised.

In constructing this critical biography, I want to acknowledge the chronicling by *Right On!*, *Word Up!*, *The Agenda*, *The City Sun*, *Rap Sheet* and other publications that have covered hiphop with the faith that it told a larger story. I hope my regard does justice to the art and the people who love it. These would include the life-savers behind this book: Barbara Zitwer, a one-woman advance team; Marilyn Wright, who offered editorial insight; Stella Kane, who respected my cultural vision enough to publish it; and Eric Lawrence and Dennis Myers, who supplied the wherewithal. Extra encouragement came from Richard Hecht, who showed patience and support, Gregory Solman, Benj DeMott and Jerry Green. And thanks to Keith Gardner, Veronica Mixon and Robert Lazzaro. I gratefully dedicate this book to young people, Tupac fans or not, who keep widening their perspectives: to Teofilo Colon and to my other nieces and nephews.

Afeni Shakur at a Black Panther press conference, 1970

Chapter One

Memories of Overdevelopment

'I want to be a revolutionary!' ten-year-old Tupac said to
Reverend Herbert Daughtry. Not too many years later, Tupac's
yearning would take him to acting school, where his radical
zeal would be encouraged. But as a respectful youngster,
mindful of his elders, Tupac answered Daughtry's inquiry
about his ambitions boldly, with all the self-assurance of a
prodigy. Revolutionary status was his goal.

It was the early eighties and attending Daughtry's The House
of the Lord Church in Brooklyn, New York, with his mother,
Afeni, and his sister, Asantewaa, gave Tupac a traditional African
American grounding, part of the upbringing that many Black
families felt necessary to establish moral boundaries and
encourage stable goals for their children. The Gospel quote,
'Teach a child the way that he should go, and when he is old he
shall not depart from it,' is a familiar axiom of Black American
family life. Anyone who has listened to the records Tupac made

as a rap artist can hear 'the way that he should go' in echoes of Gospel oral tradition. Rap's exceptional verbal command also indicates a familiarity with – an indoctrination in – methods of articulation and, especially, the command of emotional sincerity. Tupac learned in church how to mean what you say. In answering Reverend Daughtry's inquiry about his future by saying he aspired to be 'a revolutionary,' he knew he would provoke a surprised but approving response. A boy courts the favor of adults by exemplifying and repeating their own pet notions. Daughtry had long been advocating community action and boldness. Seeing his own enthusiasms reflected back to him in a shining, earnest young face placed him firmly among Tupac's very first audiences.

At the September 20, 1996 memorial service for Tupac held at The House of the Lord Church, Reverend Daughtry recounted that moment mournfully: 'Afeni brought him, along with his sister, Asantewaa, to this holy place. The three of them stood right there at the altar and united with this congregation. He was a lad of about ten years. When I asked him what he wanted to be he replied, "a revolutionary." Needless to say, I was surprised. I ought not to have been. There is a saying concerning "a chip off the old block," and "the twig doesn't fall far from the tree." His mother, Afeni, who was pregnant with him while incarcerated for allegedly plotting to bomb something – later found not guilty – was a revolutionary. She was a member of the Black Panther party, a group of young Black men and women who, some years ago, created enormous fear among some whites and a certain kind of Black.

'Afeni was committed to making things better for the masses. She was a revolutionary. If revolution means complete changes, she wanted that. Afeni wanted a complete change for the better and she thought that could happen with the Black Panthers. Later she was to fall on hard times, but we are not here to tell her story. We're here to remember Tupac. Tupac the revolutionary. He said, "I want to be a revolutionary." Maybe that explains his life.'

Daughtry's eulogy gave religious and political parallels that are as important to consider in searching for an understanding of Tupac's young life as any of its mundane incidents. The boy absorbed the idea of revolution as a goal, much the way children at Sunday School absorb the Ten Commandments, but he kept his eyes on a worldly prize with almost religious zeal.

'After he joined the church,' Daughtry continued, 'he played as any normal child. He laughed. He cried. He played with other children.' It was a childhood resonant with the contradictions – the joys and woes – of a changing America. A revolution was taking place quietly in Tupac's head and the world around him, a revolution unlike any Afeni would have sanctioned.

In 1981, as the Reagan era's mean-spirited policies began polarizing the nation between power and poverty, Afeni sought the ministry of an activist preacher like Daughtry. She was aware that her young warrior would need a double-tiered spiritual education. Daughtry knew his way around the community structures of Black Brooklyn: how to use the media to expose his congregation's problems and provoke a response to their needs. He would be pleased to find a young parishioner who also seemed to have his mind on change.

Although activism had quietened down through the relatively complacent seventies, Black America found itself confronting new social challenges that threatened to reignite the rage that had exploded in the sixties. Young Tupac's dream of revolution stood out – a rare raised fist among the millions of kiddie hands clutching Pac-Man joysticks. His answer to Reverend Daughtry reflects Afeni's experience and her soberly adjusted attitude toward social change – his mother's son's loyalty mixed with an early sense of inherited mission. A child of the revolution that never got televised, Tupac Amaru – which translates as 'shining serpent,' a reference to an insurrectionist South American warrior (the Arabic name 'Shakur' means 'Thankful to God') – was part of the new generation who were given Afro-centric names but would have to search for their emotional identities in an era of unprecedented temptation. The claim Tupac made to Daughtry was a testament to his role models; the revolutionary idea had got through to him despite the eighties' general emphasis on accommodation and reward.

Tupac listened, observed and absorbed. His bright eyes reflected a generation alert to the culture and the times. What he sensed was the skid that was taking place on the road to social equity. When Reagan smashed the air traffickers' strike, his unprecedented action produced a shudder among people brought up to believe in ideas of fair wages, workers' integrity and the hope the unions had represented for more than five decades. A new desperation was creeping in. Something cold was undercutting the hot passions of righteous activism that had enflamed the previous generation of Black youth, tempering the lessons Afeni exemplified and that Daughtry endowed with higher moral purpose. Afeni's dreams – like the beliefs of so many parents teaching their children through the mythology of ideas and helping them make sense of their everyday endeavors and set-backs – was being undermined by a coarsening social temper.

One of the delusions of the Dr Spock generation is that children can be sheltered from the world's harsh and bewildering realities. But the surprising candor and realism heard in many rap records prove otherwise – a child's sensitive awareness is part of growing up. Information about the world is pointlessly hidden from children because they seek it out and the world imposes its hard truths anyway.

Through shared language and daily media bombardment, American childhood is imprinted with the spirit of the times. To an individual for whom all things are new, an amoral education takes place, jumbling sentimental notions with brutal logic to create an image of the way the world works.

Childhood pleasure struggles with practicality. It can either be unnerving or fulfilling to imagine how a child will acquire the necessary balance. During daily subway rides and walks through New York, the sight of homelessness, deprivation and violence prompted Tupac to ask his mother, 'Why?' Afeni's replies must have been tempered to instill hope as well as resolve. She needed to give her child a sense of worth, balancing the joy they found among family and friends with the encroaching poverty and problems of post-Panther life.

Probably the only child who understands the relation between pleasure and struggle is an artistic one. Observing the aggression and rage, the intensity of New York life that makes all frantic and frenzy seem natural, or at least unchangeable, Tupac may have been affected, but it was theater school that shaped his intensity. Exposure to expressive arts gave rein to his imagination and to the dramatization of whatever impulses, convictions or confusions he felt. Studying drama also inspired his creative approaches, which included writing.

Reverend Daughtry spoke of Tupac's play-writing efforts: 'Tupac told me of one play in particular. A young man was running away from hit men and ran into this house, where he hid out; and on and on it went and when he was through I said to him, "Why not have the young man go into a church, and have a minister to help him?" He paused, he thought, he looked at me and said, "That's a good idea. You see, I have to write what I know about, what I have lived, I don't know anything about the church or religion."'

Afeni enrolled Tupac in a Harlem theater group, the 127th Street Ensemble. At the age of twelve, his first performance took place at the Apollo Theater in a production of Lorraine Hansberry's play about a Black Chicago family planning to escape urban poverty by moving to an all-white suburb, *A Raisin in the Sun*. Tupac had the kid's role, Travis, the son of Walter Lee Younger, who witnesses a microcosm of Black American social striving. Travis's most important moment paralleled Tupac's own life. He is brought to the center of the family turmoil, silently put in place by his strong-willed grandmother, who demands the boy's father act on principle so that his son can observe the proper code of behavior:

> I've come from five generations of people who was slaves and sharecroppers, but ain't nobody in my family never let nobody pay them no money that was a way of telling us he wasn't fit to walk the earth. We ain't never been that poor, we ain't never been that dead inside. No, Travis, you stay right here. And you make him understand what you're doing, Walter Lee. You teach him good like Willie Harris taught you. You show where our five generations done come to. Go ahead, son.

Such a play – such a moment – forces a knowledge on the actor as it does on the audience. Playing Travis added to Tupac's sense of alienation. It gave a deeper purpose to the extracurricular activity of acting, making use of his dawning sense of injustice, leading him to a more serious appreciation of childhood than his street-running peers, who often taunted him for his 'difference.' 'This is something that none of them kids can do,' Tupac proclaimed, proud of his sophisticated skill, yet revealing his adolescent pain and uncertainty. 'I didn't like my life, but through acting I could become somebody else.'

A southern shift would enhance that perception. In 1985, Afeni moved the family from New York to Baltimore. Hardship instigated the change, but there was also man trouble and, in the city itself, the atmosphere of atrophy. As an ex-Panther, Afeni watched, through the seventies and into the eighties, as conditions for Black America worsened, particularly in New York, with its ethnic divisions and municipal power splits that repeatedly excluded Black citizens. Starting out in the Bronx, she had shuttled her family from borough to borough. An exasperated Mother Courage, she began to understand the allure that the South held for many northern Blacks. Northern life – with its post-World War II promise of jobs and opportunity – began to pall as the nation changed and the economy supported fewer opportunities for a working-class livelihood.

Urban Baltimore's large Black population and its unique half-Southern small-town scale, its alternately charged yet docile pace, helped soothe the family's agitation. Tupac attended Rolling Park Junior High up to the eighth grade, improvising, making the kind of adjustments and facing the kind of disorientation that army brats experience when their parents are constantly forced to relocate.

It was only with his admittance to the Baltimore School of the Arts that the dreaming revolutionary found a structured outlet for his energy. In teaching styles of expression, BSA accepted random switching of identities and play-acted emotional intensity. Among the students, disputes and infatuations could be playfully explored as in musical chairs. In contrast to the Bronx's school of swift kicks, Tupac found himself enrolled in what modern America – with its downsizing of federal interest, shrinkage of government funds allocated to education and massive cutting of school appropriations – would come to see as an increasingly rare opportunity to learn and experiment. Once imagination was sparked, Tupac's creativity bloomed. 'That school was saving me, you know what I'm sayin'? I was writing poetry and shit, and I became known as MC New York, because I was rapping and then I was doing the acting thing.'

Tupac's rap vocation came as a part of the intensified growth spurt that many early eighties teens were experiencing. This was also a period of grassroots renaissance in those north-east enclaves like the Bronx and New Jersey, where rap began. A Baltimore friend was fatally shot while playing with guns – a now frequent gun-culture tragedy, at the time it was the start of a new dread reality spreading through American cities. Part of what gave hiphop appeal was its recognition of such savage realities. The mainstream rarely recognized or tried to make sense of the drugs and violence sweeping the inner cities. It would take a cultural revolution like hiphop – with Black kids putting their daily lives into their own narrative terms – to express this disturbing new reality. It was an experience that only Martin Scorsese, in his 1969 film *Who's That Knocking at My Door?*, had touched on before when he portrayed a room of fitful young (white) men toss a weapon among them in a slow-motion orgy of danger and risk, as the camera tracks the abject fear or hilarity on each random face. In that movie, Scorsese anticipates the complications of hiphop culture spiked with hazardous social rituals – the compulsion to flaunt arms – that accrue to urban male adolescence. Musical dread. It found its way into an early Tupac rhyme.

Gun in my hand / Bullets in motion /Crushin' like crumbs / The maniac psycho / Makes the bloods all run

Gun control thus became the subject of the first rap Tupac performed in Baltimore. He responded in his generation's natural terms but also, for perhaps the only time, his rap accepted the taboos of the older generation. Achieving continuity with adults did more than stroke his young ego; Tupac also took artistic assurance from it. Speaking of this period, he said, 'It was a whole other experience for me to be able to express myself – not just around Black people but also around white people and other kinds of people. It was the freest I ever felt in my life.'

The accent was on youth and young people were eager to educate and exploit themselves, with all the highs and lows that implies. Tupac's classmates exhibited a singular kind of self-taught pride in their ability to signify and vent – a pride tinged with adolescent arrogance. Attending Baltimore School of the Arts after the 1980 release of the film *Fame*, which romanticized the exploits of teens in New York's High School of the Performing Arts, would have felt like a journey toward the mecca of one's desires and ambitions. Encouraged to see themselves as special, these kids got a compounded sense of self-worth at a school that catered to the belief in unique talent.

This was where Tupac met the aspiring actress Jada Pinkett and they began kindred careers. As childhood photos attest, Tupac was a darkly handsome boy and Pinkett a light-skinned looker. As teens both were physically striking. They had trim figures, and could bat long lashes over large, direct eyes that didn't hesitate to meet another's gaze. Tupac and Pinkett must have found each other – and a lifelong friendship – in that uneasy and conflicting fellowship of adolescent narcissism and self-regard.

In the way that Tupac's motor constantly seemed to be running and in the snapping alertness that makes Pinkett a riveting if not always convincing actress, they invented their own street stardom. Playing an odd riff on Muhammad Ali's sixties pride, they created a new, hiphop style centered on perpetual preening whether there was a party, a class exercise, a stage competition or not.

These intensely social exercises in self-testing, self-consciousness and self-promotion are part of the universal teenage experience – a transition wherein the dull familiarity of family life is traded for the excitement of new friends, worldliness and independence. For Tupac this meant something of a respite from his mother's legacy of activism and the male figures darting in and out of his life – uncertain choices for role models. Theater – specifically the fun and interplay of performing – offered him a world away from home. Always 'on,' Tupac could escape the day-to-day trials his mother was facing to support her children. He found independence and flirtation, too.

Tupac and Pinkett paired up well in this teenage idyll. Both gifted, both extrovert, they could seem to be challenging whoever else was around them. It's in drama school that one learns to make use of the buried insecurities that inspire outsize expression and the need for attention-grabbing. Tupac and Pinkett practiced *Fame*'s secret motivation: putting impudence on the surface to cover up the fear underneath. Notice – acclaim – is then the reward that bolsters self-confidence. In theater it is not uncommon for such behavior and technique to become the basis of a style. It explains part of what one could call Tupac's and Pinkett's star quality: out to

9

make something of themselves by any means necessary, their sexuality is joined to will – as sixties student activist Stokely Carmichael defined it, the will not to be deterred.

Some years later, Tupac confided to the European press about his *Fame*-like days, 'I felt like I was out of place. I learned a good admiration for the real world 'cause it was different cultures, different people. I saw females kissing females, males kissing males, so it really wasn't a big thing to me [later on] when everybody was tripping off homosexuality. I already saw that in my school.'

Role-playing for the young thespian meant learning to trip off certain ideas of Black masculinity, appropriate behavioral tips for the young mover who refuses to be tricked. It's not surprising then that Afeni's son should emerge from theater school with a defiant spirit that made Carmichael (who was eventually to take the name Kwame Ture) glad to observe, 'One of the most promising developments in the nation today is the new mood among Black college students, who have long formed a conservative group with standard Horatio Alger dreams, imitating white America at its worst. Agitation on black campuses in 1967 was profound and different from that of 1960–61; there is today less of a moral and more of a political orientation. Humble appeal is gone; a powerful mood has developed based on a black consciousness.'

But Tupac's generation – his acting-out class – turned Ture's prophecy upside down. Tupac learned an impatient, multi-source agitation (from both the holy church and the wicked state) that, without a common moral impetus, at least proved to be political – though, perhaps, not moral. He preferred action; but in action without introspection, agitation turns back on itself. Rebellion for the hell of it. The impulse to speak out and strike out does little to resolve disquiet. It reflects a demand for answers that is inherent in youth's ingenuous bluster and attack, a demand that is all too easily rejected by older listeners who have forgotten their own adolescent anxiety – an adolescence spent in a clearer, more defined, more active, 'mo' better' past that rap itself now rhapsodizes about.

Pay attention to what the hiphop generation feels. It's poignantly clear in what they say even when they say it in ways that confound expectations. Music is a key. Teens' love for rap in the early eighties was indeed special. They had discovered the value of music to express identity and feeling – their own form of theater. But by the mid-nineties, hiphop had foundered. The drastic turn toward gangsta became more of an industry standard than a cultural absolute. Then, a new set of rap songs appeared, creating a virtual subgenre to the prevailing gangsta fantasy. It clues one in to what ideas and longings were also in Tupac's head during that time between acting school and rap recording. In the mid-nineties, like most of his peer group hiphop heads, Tupac grooved to Pete Rock and C. L. Smooth's 'Reminisce,' Ahmad's 'Back in the Day,' Coolio's 'I Remember' and Wu Tang Clan's 'It Was All So Simple,' each record a nostalgic ode to the rappers' remembered innocence – a not-so-distant ante-youth. These records confessed a heartfelt simplicity at odds with the reckless rage of gangsta rap. Coolio's reference to The Intruders' 'Cowboys to Girls' and Wu Tang Clan's re-working of the Gladys Knight version of 'The Way We Were' (released when Tupac and Wu Tang were preschoolers, so it seems like a strain of genetic memory) reveal a sincerity and open-heartedness that is part of these young artists' relationship to the past. Focusing on family cohesion, better days, fun without stress, the songs pose – by sheer contrast – questions about their current lives.

Hiphop nostalgia spins a subtle response to the facts of life that may appear harsh and intractable. (Looking back on the North from his new home in Baltimore, Tupac could affirm the sentiment expressed by his buddies in Live Squad's 'Heartless' and its memorable line: 'See what happens to your life when you're born in New York!') Remembrance of times past and the longing for peace, even if conjured in affected memory – these are feelings Tupac shared. The flavor of seventies Black pop – a generally agreed-upon glory decade – is at the heart of most of these hiphop references. It suggests, 'Once there was something better. We *felt* better. Society had not yet abandoned us.'

This yearning for what Ahmad calls 'the years when I was raised' – what those gruff Wu Tang adepts recognize as a mere yesterday – differs from the exhaustion of adult nostalgia. It is symptomatic of the unbearable stress young people face today as never before. In an appropriately weary way, hiphop idealizes a childhood that never really was, painting the past to make it seem positively serene. And because of this, it is possible to understand that hiphop – despite its exaggerated brutishness – contains an effort to retrieve soul. Tupac the acting student had to be aware of the motivation to make a virtue out of what, in modern America, had been deemed inhuman and unsalvageable. As Wu Tang prove, the hardest kid feels it, even as they recall their strung-out parents' past as the set-up for their own rebellion. Retrieving soul means recollecting something real. The child who attempts to make a new world from his parents' past is a homegrown revolutionary.

Tupac with Jada Pinkett © Tom Rodriquez/Globe Photos

Chapter Two

Rewind to Birth

Tupac looked back on his early days, saying, 'Yeah, we didn't have any lights at home in my house. No lights, no electricity, and I'm Bad by L. L. Cool J came out and I had batteries in my radio. I heard it for the first time and I was writing rhymes by candlelight and I knew I was gonna be a rapper.'

This moment of ironic nostalgia – juxtaposing absolute poverty and vaunting ambition – marks a turning point and reveals one crucial source of Tupac's all-or-nothing attitude. California friends said he loved Ahmad's record and cracked a laugh at the lines, 'I think I was about ten / One of those happy little niggas singing the blues.' It's more than a genre reference – or a contradiction; it implies the inheritance of not just a musical style but also an outlook. 'Blues' is as much a part of the universality of childhood as the playtime possessions made from household items.

Ecstasy, security, utopia, revenge – art is a way to deal with even the teenage blues. Tupac had made an unusual trial run at the Baltimore School of the Arts, where – as hiphop commanded more of the world's attention, attracting media interest and churning up controversy – young folks prepared to shock the world by making art of their lives.

Tupac was seventeen when Public Enemy's *Yo! Bum Rush the Show* and 'Bring the Noise' and L. L. Cool J's *Radio* and *Bigger and Deffer* made their impact. The advent of rap was an undeniable cultural landmark – a breakthrough. Its witty plain-talk on the darkest, deadliest urban woes was what Tupac called 'representing the real.' To young audiences alienated from the mainstream, rap was simply a depiction of the life they knew. A drama student could intuit the relation between this pop revolution and the historical importance of theater. Both art forms demonstrated ingenuity in addressing listeners and letting them use words and music for their own means. Tupac admired hiphop because, like Black theater, it did not seek to please only the élite and snobbish. It was unique in its lack of an authoritarian's voice. It stood for good times, being alive, for doing all the things your parents told you not to. Tupac and his friends thrilled to L. L. Cool J's 'I'm Bad' for the way it struck a tone that was neither for nor against established morals but simply against following anyone else's rules.

Because young Black artists could intuit the potential for something completely new in such records as 'The Breaks,' 'The Message' and 'Bring the Noise,' rap itself would become a theater with enormous appeal, a young person's art form based on young people's relationships and experience. Speaking informally, rap commanded language to organize a dramatic form of artist-to-audience communication. Through compelling language and/or the force of the performer's personality, rap shuttled between declaiming and confiding its ideas. It represented a collective dialogue based on an inner-city insider's understanding – an American kid's inheritance and a soon-to-be-accepted theatrical method.

Irresistibly drawn to rap, Tupac was blessed with the ability to express his feelings as charismatic conviction. His enthusiastic response to the world was forming, adding skillful elocution to his impetuous ingenuity. Commanding adolescent lingo and style was just part of it: his energy and personal charm convinced spellbound classmates that a chaotic personality was coherent.

Years later, Tupac used the language of theater to talk about hiphop's uniqueness: 'It brought me to myself,' he said, as gratefully as an actor discussing a Method breakthrough. 'Now I have a different philosophy. Hiphop, when it started, it was supposed to be the new thing that had no boundaries and was so different to everyday music. As long as the music has the true to the heart soul, it can be hiphop. As long as it has soul to it, hiphop can live.'

There's a blues-like faith in art and principle, a quintessential Black American feeling, but the key to Tupac's appeal is found in his drive and charisma – a personal image that mixes sincerity with truth, cunning with charm, and rebellious anger with acting. Tupac's journey from revolutionary to performer is a struggle to summon enough guile, nerve and enthusiasm to do his Panther legacy – and the secret intelligence of Black show business – proud.

This legacy was passed on by Afeni Shakur, the young woman who joined the Black Panthers in 1968 when she was twenty-two years old and gave birth to Tupac in a maternity ward of New York University Hospital on June 16, 1971. Only a month before, she had been released from the Women's House of Detention in Greenwich Village, after serving time, while pregnant, for her suspected part in an alleged Panther plot to bomb banks and department stores.

Afeni has spoken passionately about the Tupac pregnancy: 'I had a million miscarriages, you know. This child stayed in my womb through the worst possible conditions. I had to get a court order to get an egg to eat every day. I had to get a court order to get a glass of milk every day – you know what I'm saying? I lost weight, but he gained weight. He was born one month and three days after we were acquitted. I had not been able to carry a child. Then this child comes and hangs on and really fights for his life.'

Such intricate emotions and motivations are among the revelations of Black American life that the hiphop era has helped make clear. In this case it reveals Afeni's seemingly paradoxical trust in radical social solutions and divine beneficence.

Tupac's father, Billy Garland, another Panther party member, was not a part of Afeni's life at the time of birth (and would not be in Tupac's for at least twenty years), but both parents knew the tensions of life in stark contrast to the sanitized image of all-American comfort and contentment. Young Black Americans of that period warmed to political consciousness as an undisputed truth – a cold, clear, *better* way of looking at the world. Their shared optimism and belief that change could be accomplished created a new romanticism. Their vantage point was seventies New York – the Harlem, Brooklyn and New Jersey neighborhoods that made up a New Man's Land of social transition. Decades after the Harlem Renaissance, years after the Black Arts Movement that saw a sixties renaissance in the social beliefs and artistic ambitions of New York's urban disenfranchised and intellectuals, the place was edging almost imperceptibly into the desolation that many knew would necessitate some desperate effort to stave off. It would take personal measures, newly imagined inside political ones. Young Black people in the early seventies faced truth in the form of awakening to a rising national apathy. Making love or having a baby in this climate could seem brave or foolhardy.

Despite their eventual separation, Afeni and Billy were connected by a genuine cultural sensibility. It was the post-riots period when they met – hearts on fire like Watts, Detroit and Newark – a time when it was possible to fall in love with the buoyancy with which a puffed-out Afro hairstyle was worn or the pride implicit in the way a warrior medallion hung around the neck. Emboldened by the imperatives of the Civil Rights era that had shown, for almost two decades, how Black Americans deserved equal rights but must actively pursue them – perhaps even fight for them given the stubborn violence of racist tradition – young folks believed that they could change things.

This daring move toward change and justice was part of the impulse behind Afeni's interest in the Black Panthers. Started in the late sixties as a grassroots movement in Oakland, California, by two young men, Huey P. Newton and Bobby Seale, the Panthers sought to redress the wrongs suffered at the hands of local police, who patrolled their communities like the sentries of an occupying army. The Panthers created a new model of youthful rebellion that spoke to a wearied people's frustration and political impatience. Signing on to this resistance movement, Afeni and Billy were drawn toward activist solutions and thus each other.

Afeni had already been arrested in 1969 for conspiracy to bomb public places in New York. She began her involvement with Garland while out on bail, also meeting a second man, a local hood known by the name 'Legs.' Whether renegade or criminal, all shared concepts of political truth and social justice. In that churning atmosphere, the pop music boom represented a tidal shift. Every kid whose heart rises to the sound of a particular song on the radio knows the excitement of this kind of culture quake. In the sixties, it happened simultaneously with – and as an expression of – changing social attitudes. All across America, from Oakland to Detroit to New York, Huey Newton's arrest could inspire local graffiti artists to spray FREE HUEY messages to the world. Likewise, there was a rare enthusiasm in the way a song of this period connected with public feeling, with what young people had in their hearts that the world had previously ignored. The joy of a great song swept across the nation on the heels, toes, snapping fingers and swiveling hips of improvised dance steps.

Along with this musical explosion, new potential shone in

the way Berry Gordy Jr, a young Black entrepreneur, and his gathered-together youthful talents from Detroit's auto factories and public schools, presented them to the public in a corporate parallel to the new Black initiatives of the Civil Rights Movement. When Brenda Evans, Billy Calvin and Joe Harris – a trio of high-school vocalists full of sophomoric effrontery and cleansing, new-broom charm – made it into Motown, they awarded themselves the revolutionary title The Undisputed Truth and launched their debut single, 'Smilin' Faces (Sometimes).'

Such an R&B hit contains the substance of a social era as well as a key to comprehending the future that developed from it. Hiphop's spiritual and musical origins are as traceable as the romantic and practical origins of Tupac's life. Both can be found in 'Smilin' Faces (Sometimes),' a cultural touchstone in 1971. No intelligent young adult could pass through that time and remain unmoved by the song. Number Two in the pop charts, Number One R&B, it provided a soundtrack – a background for thinking and loving, for being and protesting the way idealistic young Afeni and Billy Garland did.

Afeni must have been particularly susceptible to musical charm. After all, her parents had christened her Alice Faye Williams, after the personable blond, forties band-singer and movie star. Certainly, Afeni was aware of the irony when she changed her own name and chose that of an Incan warrior for her child, choices suggesting matters of cultural affinity and changeable political patterns in the history of Black American living that go deeper into the essence of Black life than mere detail can impart. There is more to gain from knowing that Afeni came from a background open to the delight of Alice Faye singing 'This Year's Kisses' than from a list of bland parental activities. American pop history abounds with such rich paradoxes.

Who could resist The Undisputed Truth? The group's two Black men and one Black woman sang ardor and insight for before The Fugees, a similarly constituted nineties group, were even gleams in their parents' eyes. The Undisputed Truth used conversational interplay both between the sexes and within a community. Singing in whispers, tremors and startled exhortations, they communicated distress, a shared alarm in which each of the three singers confirms the sadness and the wisdom of the others so that none of them is ever alone. You can hear traces of this style in the way Tupac himself trades verses with K-Ci on 'I Ain't Mad at Cha' and in the vocals of Bone Thugs-N-Harmony.

A reversal takes place, in this song, of the previous standard of Black pop male–female singing – the cheerily bourgeois The Fifth Dimension who made up for their approximation of the Ray Coniff Singers' bland harmonics with the startling, chicly Black, long-hot-summer urbanity of 'Stone Soul Picnic' (1969). The Fifth Dimension's new Black cachet retrieved their lost relevance in the ghetto (the word had just become popular because of student activist usage). They grabbed it from a distance and with kid gloves, like the long arm of a parvenu snatching crumbs of soul food from a picnic table as the record company limousine zooms them through the inner city en route to the suburbs. Something genuinely, inherently ethnic is in 'Stone Soul Picnic' – it evokes family reunion and street corner jive but sung in a gospel-like chorale. (That's why Crystal Waters would cover it with popular success in 1993.)

Part of the wonder of the era was that bourgies could achieve such clout. In the song, those high-gloss repetitions of that other newly coined phrase 'soul' (even as Florence La Rue and Marilyn McCoo made each utterance crystalline) ˄unded authentic. It locked The Fifth Dimension in place as ˄ &B group – justified, no longer dismissed. Even radical ˄ists got the message of unity in the arch declamations ˄oul Picnic,' it being no less redolent of Black ˄ecisely, Black career luck) than the way The ˄ distilled five-part harmonics into three-part

Following quickly on Marvin Gaye's landmark 1970 album, *What's Goin' On*, this ethnic-specific approach wasn't exactly unheard of in pop, but it had a new feel. Suddenly, The Undisputed Truth was facing up to nihilism and defying it in fascinating, soul-deep ways. By darkening The Fifth Dimension's complacency and glee, their satisfied sense of settling for mainstream America's standards, The Undisputed Truth acknowledged in its stead the fresh acceptance of a bold new standard – a sense of in-your-face reality that opposed middle-class, establishment-pleasing niceties that were the model for The Fifth Dimension's crossover success. The name 'Undisputed Truth' presupposes an argument won. It carries the suggestion of a rebuttal, then dismisses it. Such unfazed debate would have intrinsic appeal to the stressed insistence of young activists like Afeni Shakur's Black Panthers, who were used to having their words and deeds disputed by outsiders and, by 1971, from within the ranks. For Afeni, who had distanced herself from Billy Garland when the infatuation faded and other Panther men came to suit the seriousness of her need, the song could be heard as an indicator of underground ruminations and imminent discord.

Such aggrieved entertainment is one of the defining glories of post-World War II pop culture. The song was co-written by former vocalist Barrett Strong, who sang (and co-penned with Berry Gordy in 1960) Motown's first hit, 'Money,' the signature ode of urban Black America's strivings. Strong and Gordy were trailblazers at updating blues expressions. One reason there was never a North–South rivalry among sixties Black artists as there was between east–west nineties artists, was the recent memory of what South-to-North migration meant for Black Americans, who were simply aiming at survival wherever they could find a job. A living sense of history bound them, as did respect for the musical interplay heard in superficially diverse 'soul' vs. 'pop' styles. Motown artisans were connoisseurs of blues fundamentals. Knowing that the same American racial experience underpinned both styles, sixties and seventies Black artists left rivalry to journalists and enjoyed the insights pop offered, and the assurance felt from blues resonances. Motown was able to vary Black pop's references by including northern urbanity in song subjects but southern vocal depth in the sound of Black pop. By the late sixties, pioneer Strong had begun a songwriting partnership with an in-house Motown genius, Norman Whitfield; their collaboration resulted in at least two masterpieces, 'Smilin' Faces (Sometimes)' and The Temptations' 'Just My Imagination.'

Whitfield, a producer of exhilarating records, the Hank Shocklee of his day, specialized in rough, atmospheric, almost three-dimensional soundscapes to balance his own melodic romantic tendencies – innate genius checking and balancing the slick technique he developed at Gordy's song factory, dubbed Hitsville, USA. With Strong providing a sturdy yet deluxe shell, Whitfield could experiment with the far side of the Black unconscious – not just proverbial lust and longing, but suppressed rage and despair – and make it go pop. The string glissando on 'Just My Imagination' is the sourest irony. It mocks the ecstasy so frequently sung about in Motown hits, especially those nonpareil Smokey Robinson tunes to which The Temptations gave exquisite voice. By the end of the sixties, Whitfield and Strong had the Temps earnestly parodying their own winsome selves. 'Just My Imagination' remakes Langston Hughes's 1951 'A Dream Deferred' (from the poem 'Harlem,' which also provided the title for *A Raisin in the Sun*) as if in a Detroit Cadillac plant. Hughes's protest comes off the assembly line sparkling, but revved up with a deeper ache from two more decades of wound, rot, burden – now ready to explode, as his poem predicted. He wasn't just speaking of Black distress, but anticipating a culture-wide explosion that Motown ironically named 'The Sound of Young America,' the company's brash motto.

'Just My Imagination' turns Black despair into everybody's lament. Disguised as a love song, there is politics in the Whitfield–Strong deferred dream – the equality struggled for remains just out of reach, like an idealized love object. In the early seventies, mention of an unobtainable ideal alluded to so many dissatisfactions and heartaches that each listener could hear the song a particular way in his/her heart, while the great unified understanding of it was as an elevated romantic plaint. Such a pop gift served Whitfield and Strong well in another collaboration, the explicitly socially aware 'Ball of Confusion,' a psychedelicized version of white sixties protest anthems like Barry McGuire's 'Eve of Destruction.' Motown's awareness phase could transcend trendiness with sheer oomph, as 'Ball of Confusion' proved but 'Smilin' Faces (Sometimes)' did it better by insinuating dis-ease.

No longer joyful, this Black protest admits a new social element of pop paranoia that would lie in wait until rap. The pop world of 1971 didn't know what it was getting in the bass notes and lowering tempos of 'Smilin' Faces (Sometimes),' its stark interjections piercing the strong male lead as the trio strains not to lose the murky melody. Its sinister sound mixed with Tupac's birth cries.

> *Smilin' Faces (Sometimes)*
> *Pretend to be your friend*
> *Smilin' Faces*
> *Show no traces*
> *Of the evil that lurks within*

Whitfield's production was anticipating the multi-level effects of hiphop. But even more, it gives a sensitive record of the breakdown in social confidence. Peace, Love and Harmony are just in the singer's imagination. Pain, Betrayal and Disappointment are the harsh reality. The piquant female lines give a sexy aura – a sign that Black women feel this hurt, too; a suggestion that the family, the community, are going through hell *together*, making this one of pop's most wised-up love songs – and one of the bitterest since those sung by Billie Holiday. Its splendid cynicism matches some post-riot, post-

Cointelpro Black Panther party outrage.

Afeni's involvement with the 'New York 21' Panthers, accused of planning to bomb public spaces, was central to the party's eventual dissolution. (Imprisoned on more than 200 charges, she later defended herself and was acquitted.) The party's splintered objectives over mission, strategy and conduct dashed specific Black hopes for revolution *and* camaraderie. It was lyrically codified in a New York 21 letter sent to Panther headquarters in Oakland, accusing the party's West Coast branch of 'tripping out, pseudo-machoism, arrogance, myrmidonism, dogmatism, regionalism, regimentation and fear . . . ' That letter proved somebody in the New York 21 had verbal skills, and used them to express the same internal struggle between pretense and sincere despair that echoes in:

> *The truth is in my eyes*
> *Cuz my eyes don't lie*
> *Amen*
> *Remember, a smile is just a frown*
> *Turned upside down*
> *My friend*

That combination was both poignant and naïve in the late-Panther days, when Black youth was primed to act on the need for social change. Student protest was a sign of this urge – it wasn't just for college-privileged whites. The Student Non-violent Coordinating Committee (SNCC – a neo-logo/anagram worthy of rap's U.T.F.O. or Run-DMC) sought ways of expressing its acting out, its activism, its bitterness *and* its seriousness by upping the stakes, sharpening Civil Rights rhetoric. Free lunch programs to feed inner-city children who needed nourishment, along with an improved educational structure, proved the intelligence and effectiveness of Panther activism. Restlessly progressive, eager to provoke change, SNCC brought a special intensified purpose to the Civil Rights Movement.

When its young leader Stokely Carmichael embraced Panther ideology, he demonstrated just the sort of drive and recklessness that defined the political yearning of enlightened Black youth. Carmichael's no-nonsense intensity, combined with the theatricality of Huey Newton's, Bobby Seale's and Eldridge Cleaver's already histrionic Panthers, proved to be inflammatory. Poised in a coordinated frieze of black berets, leather, guns and flags – a quasi-military parody of American male power – young Panthers were a definitive illustration of youth's infatuation with both force and change – the wild romance of independence. Sometimes uncontrollable, this spirit is distinguished by effrontery and nerve, the kind of daring that can bring down sensible strategies of resistance or foil plans for progress. This is what happened to seventeen-year-old Jonathan Jackson, young brother of Soledad prison Panther George Jackson. Jonathan, in a move as chaotic and slapstick-futile as a future rap video routine (for example Tupac's rolling with K-Ci and Danny Boy in *Toss It Up*), attempted to break George out of jail. Cut to the aftermath: George still behind bars and two cops dead, along with one young Panther – Jonathan.

Not just a casualty of 'youth,' this tragedy specifically illustrates the danger in unchecked zeal, the raging impatience Black youth are subject to with their wet, wild passion for creating justice – even sometimes through self-destructive backlash. This spark, recurring in Tupac's own wildness, determined the Panthers' apprehensive response to the Jonathan Jackson fiasco. Whether methodical or impulsive, rational or reactionary, the loss of faith after Jonathan's flash-out singed the Panthers' most instinctive connections. The party charred, optimism fell away before suspicion. Once different styles of protest no longer coalesced, uniform principle dispersed in panic. Beset by outside investigations, the first East and West Coast rivalries posed Black youth ambitions against each other. Every discordant note rankled.

More infamously catastrophic than Jonathan's teenage

kamikaze act was the New York 21's controversial brush with celebrity. Panther party glamor – and the urgent correctness of its intensified Civil Rights push – captured the imaginations of white liberals, whose support was catalogued and ridiculed by the imperiously indifferent Tom Wolfe in *Radical Chic & Mau-Mauing the Flak Catchers*.

A social group every bit as dreamy-eyed and susceptible as youth, white liberals ignored the complications surrounding Panther activity. Acting on benevolent impulses, they threw a party for the Panther 21's court defense. But in addition to accruing Wolfe's snide distemper, the fundraiser also further estranged the East Coast Panthers from the original Oakland base. Across the nationhood of Black and white America, democracy was snapping and cracking as it went pop. Panthers who wanted social revolution now mixed with harsher radicals such as the Weathermen, extremists from the Students for a Democratic Society, whose anarchic tactics appealed to Panthers of a less tolerant, more impatient style. Passionate hubbub resulted and is perhaps best signified by a line Jane Fonda spoke at that Radical Chic gathering: 'Revolution is an act of love. We are the children of revolution, born to be rebels – it runs in our blood.' Proclaiming the Panthers 'our revolutionary vanguard,' she went on to declare, 'We must support them with love, money, propaganda and risk.'

Only a churl – and a racist one at that – could laugh at Fonda's reasoning. While the future would embarrass her naïveté, the contemporary moment had certainly ennobled it. Romance was the irreducible element that kept Panther mystique going. Even if one extends the meaning of the word to include Afeni's personal affections, romance never is far off the mark of the political nature of people's lives. That's what makes 'Smilin' Faces (Sometimes)' so uncannily expressive. The intricacy of Afeni Shakur's love life – co-parenting with Billy Garland, co-habitating with Panther Lumumba Shakur and later with the mysterious drug dealer Legs – suggests a particular neo-democratic, libertarian turmoil. Afeni at the apex of a flesh-and-blood triangle, replicates the position of the female vocalist in The Undisputed Truth, who herself symbolized the overstressed, ambivalent heart of Black America in the cloudy days after non-violence and radicalism had both peaked.

Afeni Shakur's part in the New York 21 offers a young woman's version of Jonathan Jackson's impudence. While more personally, intimately contested, her desire and ambitions still reflect a sense of desperation that had overcome the Black young adults who had seen so many of their ideals founder and dissipate. Afeni's choice of men and her commitment to fate, accident, whim and dream are unextraordinary in the life of a contemporary woman, and, therefore, are part of the common human experience that bears the influence of fashion and principle as much as of dream and depression. (Legs, the pusherman, propped her up when she couldn't stand on her own.) But Afeni, in love, lust or principle, must have felt as Jane Fonda described, only, perhaps, with more commitment. As a member of the renegade New York 21, Afeni must also have conducted her romantic revolution with a degree of fuck-it-all radicalism. She empowered herself to make bold political and sexual decisions. Panther ideology in her head, Panther loyalty in her jail cell, Panther dialectic in her bed.

'Smilin' Faces (Sometimes)' dramatizes the duplicity that shocked the Panthers in their last days. Announcing the despair that would blanket Black America at the coming dawn of crack, the song makes real and sensual the spiritual drift that the militants had protested against. Heard as serious gossip, it warns of deception and distrust. Its insinuating melody is the opposite of a political anthem, slipping fear under the listener's skin. A shared ideology (a brother- and sisterhood) is being underminded in the song's 'plot.' As male voices control this narrative, the woman's voice shakes it: 'The truth is in my eyes ... Amen.' Afeni's independence can be felt in that statement. But perfidious Eve is not the song's point; instead, the female singer subtly refuses the pressure put on her by men and circumstance. She'll give birth as her final judgment on the differences and disputes with which men, mostly, deceive.

Before rap with its harsh messages, it was impossible to imagine an R&B record with the amount of pessimism of 'Smilin' Faces (Sometimes).' (Backing vocals ask, 'Can you dig it?', preparing you for the worst that is to come. The lead male's moan, 'Oh, Lordy,' is a vestige of the Negro spiritual – yesterday's protest genre now made to sound anachronistic.) The song's realpolitik is not a matter of condemning society but a profound recognition of the failings humans are heir to.

The warnings are blunt and emphatically repeated:

> *Beware!*
> *Beware of the handshake*
> *There hides a snake*
> *Beware!*
> *Beware of the pat on the back*
> *It just might hold you back*
> *Jealousy! (Jealousy!)*
> *Misery! (Misery!)*
> *Envy! (Envy!)*

It's that New York 21 letter made public, revealing to all the dissolution of the Civil Rights Movement's camaraderie and its hopes. These are the passions – and confusion – Tupac was born into.

As a child of seventies pop, Tupac could bask in the glow of Black consciousness that that era's pop music made splendid – Curtis Mayfield's 'Don't Worry,' Marvin Gaye's 'Mercy, Mercy Me (The Ecology),' Stevie Wonder's 'You Haven't Done Nothin',' The Staple Singers' 'Respect Yourself.' If Afeni exposed her boy child to such radio waves as 'Smilin' Faces (Sometimes)' it had to be intended as an *unsentimental* *education.**But the sentiment, an enthusiasm for Black intelligence, skepticism and perseverance, still came through paradoxically in pop's trenchant swing: the flow and embrace of music, the active, rebellious potential in dancing, head-bobbing, finger-snapping.

In this way, ideas that represented the evolution of Black political protest and social enterprise became an unmistakable part of that era's popular currency. Revolt was absorbed by young minds as naturally as if it were a given of Black living habits. Spike Lee missed this insight in *Crooklyn's* story of seventies hellions, ignoring the part culture played in the formative years of his generation and how he and his siblings and contemporaries processed the images and ideas of pop's radical gestalt. What Lee and perhaps other seventies teens took for granted, Tupac's generation realized one step further as automatic, as their legacy. Lee's generation had seen just enough of Civil Rights' early, tumultuous striving, the despondency of mid-sixties riots, the shock of the decade's assassinations and the splintering of youthful outrage in

---

* For herself, Afeni could sing Cheryl 'Pepsii' Riley's 'Thank You for My Child' (1989), one of the rare songs about single parenthood to address the mixed blessing of love–abandonment–redemption. It's a rarely delineated experience that, perhaps, required the hiphop era, with its respect for the facts of life that had stigmatized the Black community, to ever be given full expression. Riley's song becomes Afeni's song because in the lyrics of a single parent's self-realization, it makes peace with the difficulty of a love relationship that doesn't last. There is forgiveness in the record, but also a stern determination to find a meaning in life – the sense to make joy and substance out of the fleeting pleasure and eventual hurt of a human liaison.

While Afeni might not quite agree with Riley's second layer of meaning that turns a mother's resignation into holy devotion – it might seem too conventional – there is, yet, sentimental certainty that Afeni, the Black American woman radical who was principled, and traditional, enough to avail herself of membership in Reverend Herbert Daughtry's House of the Lord Church in Brooklyn, relates quite passionately to Riley's praise to God. The politically conscious woman and the love-conscious young girl share the hope that a parent places in the life of a child, a hope for future companionship, for a continuation of her own line of belief and heritage.

various scarily bold groups to know what sacrifices were at stake in the Black struggle. Tupac's generation had no sense of the stake, only an awareness that some sacrifice was still being exacted – unfairly.

This corresponds to the sorrowful fact of homelessness: experience of sacrifice without an attendant, justifying purpose. Poverty and social disruption became the terms of Tupac's youth – which the exuberance of seventies pop contrasted not quite mockingly, but sardonically. By the time Tupac was five, his life had begun to mirror pop's heightened big-screen versions. Mama Afeni – her words vocalized by Gladys Knight, her avidity portrayed by Diahann Carroll in the movie *Claudine* – lived a life that delineated the funhouse distortion of great ideas into grim truth. Their mother-and-son misfortunes echoed pop depictions. For a kid raised on pop this could result only in confusion, intensified by the frustration teens feel at life's inability to imitate media fantasy. For Tupac, the conditions of poverty were surreal because their cause seemed incomprehensible and unchangeable. This would directly influence the aesthetic of Tupac's raps.

Living in a psychosocial limbo, Tupac tangled with the meanings of rootlessness as his mother moved house from the Bronx to Brooklyn, apartments to shelters, from city to city. Hints of motivation came through in the decisions to migrate – the packing up of troubles and the relocating of opportunity. But without being given an explanation, without understanding, a mobile child can only manufacture sense by developing compensatory, defensive sensibility. Tupac's was based on the one thing he was sure of – that no home, no community, no goal is certain.

His childhood in New York was shadowed by the failure of the dissolute Panthers. Along with the party's collapse, the taut communal spirit that believed in change as an improvement also evaporated. Lack of opportunity underscores this desolation; its effect on the morale of parents and neighbors seeps into a child's innocence and kills it. The support system that insures a child's spiritual growth was attenuated, in spite of a mother's best efforts to encourage and protect it.

Only naturally, the child's resilient mind rallied. Family acquaintances describe Tupac's shyness – a certain sign of an active fantasy life making up for the father–son interaction he wanted but couldn't actually accomplish. A classmate reports on Tupac's artistic interest, 'He wrote some poetry to me then. He was sincere, very sincere.'

While not the average boy–boy activity (until rap), poetry-writing typifies a mind above street level. (It was punk-infatuated Chryssie Hynde who, in 'Message of Love,' quoted Oscar Wilde: 'We are all of us in the gutter/Some of us are looking at the stars.') Poetry's ordering of words and feelings expresses a desire to remake the commonplace into an example of its transcendence. Even trite poetry – perhaps *especially* trite poetry – contains the hunger for sublimity. It would be easy to say that Tupac found his inspiration in then prevalent examples of rap DJing – the advent of Funky Four Plus One, the Treacherous Three and Sugarhill Gang made an impact, no doubt. But at ten, Tupac's impulse to write and share poetry more impressively proves a solitaire's motivation that is psyche-deep rather than fashion-slick.

Was this a grounding? Perhaps not ideal, but it's what Tupac was equipped with as he made his own lifestory in hiphop. And it explains the complicated interweave of angry suppositions, desperate rationalizations and entrancing emotional flow that ruled his life as it also shaped his lyrical content.

Press 'Play' on Tupac's 1996 recording 'I Ain't Mad at Cha' and you can hear 'Smilin' Faces (Sometimes)' echoing throughout – not in an actual musical sample, but in the suggestions of menace and distrust cutting through the urban folksiness. This is the piquant, naïve combination of theatricality and lost hope as a nineties artist would convey it. He's cut off from the roots of dislocation that inspired The Undisputed Truth, yet intent on making vivid a half-truth about the conditions of contemporary Black survival – Tupac's own – in his ambivalent oration that mixes fun with anger and despair. Afeni's generation possessed social insight too penetrating to create such ambivalence, even as a guileful dramatic stance. For Tupac, the stance was what most remained from that era's turmoil. His artistic sensibility was compelled to affect a modern posture. Revolution's love-child, Tupac gravitated toward using the slings and arrows of racist America's outrageous fortune.

Hit 'Play' again and see Tupac as a quasi-political cupid, armed with the bluff and ardor of a generation that means to do things differently, advancing on the world's stage. He's born shrewd – yet innocent.

Digital Underground

Chapter Three

East vs. Waste

'Gotta stay swift,' a West Coast acquaintance remembers Tupac saying whenever he talked about his family's constant movement, partly to show off his street smarts, partly in self-defense. Tupac never had a chance to graduate from the Baltimore School of the Arts. He was seventeen when Afeni, in flight from the troubles that had led her into crack addiction, moved her family to Marin City, on the West Coast. Tupac, who might have been dreaming of the green, sunny amenities of a California suburb, found himself a continent away from 'home,' stranded in yet another bleak, burned-out, drug-swamped urban ghetto. 'Leaving BSA affected me so much,' Tupac said later, with real sorrow. 'I see that as the point where I got off the track.' Although, for a time, Tupac attended Tamalpais High School, he didn't stay there long enough to graduate and later received a general equivalency diploma.

Those first years of Tupac's northern California sojourn

came down to scrounging for a living, selling drugs, hustling, even some family fighting with Afeni. Tupac watched a frightening cloud of despair settle over his mother – the same mood of desolation that seemed to be suffocating the West Coast community he was discovering. As the only male in the household, driven by an itching aspiration toward manhood, Tupac was in turmoil.

It wasn't long before he left home to move in with a new friend in the neighborhood. According to Reverend Daughtry, 'They said he hit bottom. He was constantly looking for a place to stay and something to eat. It seemed nobody liked him in those days, except his mother . . .'

This breakout west could be thought of as a typical on-the-road, youthful exploration – it's generally depicted as a white myth, but as it happens Black American youth dealing with the same disorientation, feeling the same need to embark on a spiritual quest, also forges its own road mythology.

Staying swift, Tupac began a moral juggling act; he sold drugs and wrote poetry. With visions of L. L. Cool J still in his head, Tupac saw in hiphop his dream of personal salvation. Leila Steinberg, the retired dancer and singer from Sonoma County who eventually became Tupac's first manager, recalled their first meeting: 'He had a real difficult living situation in Marin City and I always had the household that anybody that needed a spot or whatever came through. And so, I was [teaching arts in local school] programs, and 'Pac did some of his poetry and rapped for me. And I thought he was probably the most brilliant young poet, rapper, whatever, I'd ever heard.'

Tupac circled around Marin City rap culture as an answer to his rootlessness. Steinberg had another ambitious youngster working with her, Ray Luv, and soon Tupac and Luv became part of the short-lived six-member group Strictly Dope, performing at local clubs and house parties, struggling to produce a demo that might lead to a record deal. When they announced plans to go professional, Tupac and Luv turned to Steinberg, asking her to manage them. Not feeling up to it, she turned them down. 'Well, you're gonna,' Tupac insisted. 'I already see it. You would be the best manager.' And he was right. It was Steinberg who introduced Tupac and Luv to her friend Atron Gregory, who had started his own record label, TNT, featuring a local rap group, Digital Underground.

'I had a party at my house,' Steinberg recalls. 'And I made a video ... It was like the video of the artists I finally decided I was going to represent. So I made this video and sent it to Atron. And he said, "I don't know. You have to take them to Shock G from Digital, and he'll tell me if he thinks Tupac's that tight." Strictly Dope wasn't working out (Ray Luv's father didn't want him to continue the group), so Steinberg drove Tupac to Starlight Studios in Richard to meet Digital's leader, Greg Jacobs (Shock G). 'I said, "Greg, you know, I've got this artist and you gotta hear him, 'cause I want Atron to give us a record deal." ' After spending a year trying to convince uninterested Bay area music dreamers to bet on Tupac, Steinberg finally got an audience. 'Tupac floored Greg. Completely. He was so tight.' Steinberg begged Greg Jacobs to let Tupac work with Digital and 'that's how it got started.'

With new impetus, Tupac hooked up again with Ray Luv and Strictly Dope had a brief revival – long enough for the duo to sign up with Atron Gregory's TNT Records and record some tracks under Greg Jacobs's supervision. 'That whole album is finished,' Steinberg remembers. 'That's an album that's never been released. It's Tupac's first album, as a member of Strictly Dope. Atron owns the masters and holds the right to the first album. Maybe one day he'll put it out.'

When Luv's father put pressure on his son to quit, Tupac felt the abandonment blues again. With showbiz in abeyance, his thoughts turned to education. 'I used to pull 'Pac in. I would have him help do my work in schools,' Seinberg told *4080* magazine. 'He always had this commitment to education. And I was working on curriculums, I always felt that if the curriculums were different, and people of color were represented in schools, all people of all colors, then we'd have a different society. And he always supported that.'

In limbo, Tupac considered a move to Atlanta as part of a student organization. His curiosity and restlessness had a political aspect too. In 1989, he became chairman of a group called the New African Panthers – young brothers determined to honor the goals of the original Party but not to repeat its mistakes. *Rap Sheet* magazine reported on this adventure as a brief respite from the Marin City rap race. New African Panthers' out-of-town location put Tupac on the road for a month, as he became that organization's youngest chairman to date.

In terms of cost, Tupac would trade New African Panther social activism for a newer sort that, at least in its flashiness and novelty, seemed more directly influential on the imaginations of late-eighties Black youth. There was also the promise of fun. Instead of underground political activity, Tupac was bedazzled by a new approach that parodied revolution through the subversiveness of pleasure. This was personified by Digital Underground. That Bay area rap group stressed the oldest meaning of the word 'party.' Wearing freakazoid disguises to play out the purely libidinal aspect of Black pop, they utilized the decade's infatuation with the neo-showbiz of hiphop that had revived dance music in newer, wilder styles. Digital Underground's only big hit, 'The Humpty Dance,' was a neo-pornographic commingling of eighties funk like Cameo's 'Word Up' and a hebephrenic sexual compulsion put in comical code by George Clinton's 'Atomic Dog,' but made acceptably licentious by the Prince of *Dirty Mind*. The group's name proposed a computer-age manifestation of gut-bucket secrets. Shock G, Digital Underground's lead vocalist, assumed a second role as Humpty Humpp, a *commedia dell'arte* figure with a exaggerated phallus-type nose and a distorted, nasal vocal delivery that suggested he was rapping from under the sheets.

Before 'The Humpty Dance,' rap had few actual dance cuts – Rob Base and DJ Easy Rock's sublime 'It Takes Two' was a rare hit, derived from the incessant momentum of club music. 'The Humpty Dance' retained rap's percussive, speaking rhythms and by doing so translated the dance/party ethic to hiphop. Digital Underground's energy level struck a chord with Tupac, who auditioned to join the group. His association with Greg Jacobs and Digital's other founding member, Money B, formed a bond of ambition – of like-mindedness – that was impossible to shake off. In 1990 Shock G took him on, first as a roadie, then as a dancer. Steinberg says 'Greg asked 'Pac to come on the road with him and be a dancer. And the thing was, 'Pac was always an artist in his own right. And the funny thing is, he may have been a background dancer for Digital Underground, but I swear to God he took the stage every time. He couldn't've been a background person, he out-shined everybody on every stage he was ever on. That's real.'

This was the period when rap was developing new modes of stage presentation and dancers had a fundamental role in supplying the visual excitement rappers themselves rarely provided, marching along the perimeters of the stage. At the Baltimore School of the Arts, Tupac had enjoyed some nominal ballet training, and this helped him to stay agile and keep his energy focused on creativity. The early nineties offered an unusual moment in Black male self-presentation, taking the eye-candy place showbiz usually reserved for women. But young men were able to display a different kind of Black athleticism, not dreaming of Michael Jackson/James Brown glory but dancing out the steps and body twists that came directly from the street (Oakland's MC Hammer was just about to break), representing a cultural ethos. One of John Singleton's first films was just such a video, *Steppin' into the House*, for the dance-rap group 06 Style. It overlapped low-rent images of 06 Styles' four members showing off their own choreographic charm. Tupac fell into the dance-spell for Digital Underground, but dance never satisfied his impatience. It was after his appearance on Digital Underground's *This is an EP* in 1991, in 'Same Song,' that Tupac realized the joy and fulfillment to be had in putting a rhyme on tape and out to the public.

If it hadn't been for a police incident – Tupac was stopped by police in downtown Oakland and cited not for dancing but jaywalking – the year would have been remembered as the artist's clear, hopeful send-off. Instead, his East to West journey was tainted with the suggestions of trouble ahead. Digital Underground offered platinum promise, along with a considerable fun quotient. The names of the group's production company, 'Stayin' Busy,' and writing collective, 'Underground Write-How-You-Like Regime,' (playing off code words from 'The Humpty Dance,' 'Do what you like') show their flippancy. These jokers could easily waylay a young warrior's more serious interests – or at least complicate them.

On 'Same Song' Digital Underground samples 'Theme to the Black Hole' by Parliament, with its Motown-based shuffle and thump embraced as a California response to historical Black distress – specifically, boredom. Digital Underground advises dancing as a diversion from the world's dulling repetition, the ghetto's lack of progress. But when Tupac joins the fun, his smile turns into a frown.

Here is Tupac's first mainstream rap:

> *Now I clown around*
> *When I used to hang around*
> *With the Underground*
> *Girls who used to frown*
> *Say I'm down*
> *When I come around*
> *Gas me*
> *And when they pass me*
> *They used to dis me*
> *Harass me*
> *And now they ask me*
> *If they can kiss me*
> *Get some thangs*

> *People change*
> *Want to live they life high*
> *Same song*
> *Can't go wrong*
> *If I play the nice guy*

Humpty interjects, 'Claim to fame / Must be changed / Now that we became strong.'

And Tupac finishes:

> *Parliament still the same*
> *Cuz it's the same song.*

These tracks present Tupac as a highly self-conscious nineties Candide (though his knowing smirk on 'kiss me' suggests Casanova). The chorus on 'Same Song' chants, 'Been all around the world,' bringing DJ Quik's worldly realization into Tupac's sense of the world, as if the annoying fickleness of rap's social action markedly perplexes him. His rap's awareness of public jealousy is already more substantive than Digital Underground's usual trivial subjects. Instead of not minding how he's seen, like Shock G, Tupac is aware of how he comes off, of upsetting people by his very ambition and achievement. On this professional debut, Tupac has travelled westward, from the troubled, principled East Coast to the pleasure-struck West Coast, where showbiz, or non-activism – what Afeni might consider waste – zonked him with its complicated rewards. The line 'If I play the nice guy' will become the subtext of everything else he ever recorded. Hiphop's Candide faces the first of many moral lessons. Political crisis already makes itself felt.

Afeni could sense this happening and became an interested observer of hiphop whenever there was a record that took into account the complications Black America was going through. At the time of Tupac's first record success, Afeni took note of 'a song that says something. I hear some of Tupac's stories in it.'

The reference is to DJ Quik's 'Jus Lyke Compton,' a road song that came from the new generation of rappers but also meant something to an ex-Panther who had entered the life of a road-running fugitive: 'Finally left the motherfuckin' C-P-T / Off to other cities and shit / No longer just an underground hit / Movin' things / A local nigga made good / And made a name offa makin' tapes for niggas in the 'hood / Let me tell a little story / about the places that I been to / And the shit that I been through.'

While the romance of road mobility suffuses this song, Quik's narration gets swiftly to the sobering reality of career-sanctioned 'freedom' – that lateral social movement that undermines the dream of showbiz success. 'Foolish was I to think there wasn't other cities like this / And they didn't like this,' he reasons. Any American traveling across the continent seeing the stress and squalor common to the life of our national underclass knows this let-down, and Tupac on the road felt no differently. 'Quik got it right,' he'd say while in the studio making *Strictly for My N.I.G.G.A.Z.* Quik's tune accounts for the disillusionment awaiting naïve, would-be rappers who, like Tupac, thought themselves on the road to Oz: 'That's when I started thinking this wasn't like home / But then they had to prove me wrong.'

Tupac's first stop west being northern California (coincidentally, Quik begins: 'Now Oakland is just like Compton"), the song now seems like prophecy for the area of the country that would be his post-Baltimore destination.

Spooky fate laughs in the background of Quik's odyssey, a ghostly chorus. From Oakland to St Louis, San Antonio to Denver, Quik persists in offering an observation that Tupac and all rap hopefuls would make: 'How could a bunch of niggas in a town like this / Have such a big influence on niggas so far away?' Once in Marin City, Tupac took up Quik's wondering about hiphop's expansion; he also pondered the spread of social disaster he saw everywhere he went, the radical changes neither he nor Afeni could find. The song meant much to both Tupac and Afeni because its sense of an elusive homeland makes music of the American social discomfort they were experiencing at first hand (an experience from which political commentators are so remote as they lack either personal knowledge or the simple curiosity to seek it out or address it). But the delight of this song is that emotionally – in the joy and ingenuity of Quik's rhymes, his illustrative observations, humorous details and clever asides – it makes a place of intellectual and moral stability in the art of hiphop, in the very act of rapping.

This is what Tupac meant by describing rap as 'this new thing that had no boundaries and was so different to everyday music.' It offered an alternative way of coping. In hiphop was a philosophy reborn from what Afeni knew but was central to the way Tupac's generation saw the world – particularly, how Tupac viewed the late-eighties ruins that remained of Black activism's place of origin.

Chapter Four

The B–Boy Bounce

'America's Nightmare: Mutulu Shakur, Assata Shakur'
— Tupac on 'Wordz of Wisdom'

How many Shakurs does it take to raise a child, an artist, a revolutionary? The home environment Afeni provided might have been short on material comforts but it did ensure — for a time anyway — the presence of progressive examples for her children.

Afeni had not disclosed the identity of Tupac's father but she made it clear that he was not Lumumba Shakur, who was the lead defendant in the Panther 21 case. Soon after her acquital and release from jail, Afeni moved in with Lumumba's adopted brother Mutulu. Mutulu Shakur (born Jeral Wayne Williams) — the father of Tupac's brother, Mopreme — was not a mere figurehead but a model of radicalism for the family to emulate.

Afeni's ambitious, idealized family plan was doomed by

poverty and discouragement. The domestic conventions that she had so fiercely opposed would backfire disastrously. A dire irony: family was the only means to self-sufficiency but also, inadvertently, a trap. Caught between poverty and the implicit luxury of radicalism, there wasn't adequate buttressing either from society at large or from the personal network of associations Afeni knew to make real the familial transformation she had once so passionately envisioned.

And Mutulu would be convicted for his involvement in the infamous 1981 armored-car robbery that left two Nyack, NY, policemen and a Brinks guard dead. Mutulu still claims his innocence. Taken away from the family circle, he continued to think of himself as a helpmate to the family. 'Father, friend, comrade,' is how he described his relationship to Tupac. Conversations between them were, as Tupac poignantly remembered, 'good lessons.' Histories, examples and anecdotes were passed. 'He taught me important things about loyalty, about fighting, about beliefs. All the stuff a young nigga need to know not to fall for the shit waitin' out here. Just us two, talkin'.' And relating. Until the law intervened, forcing both the growing boy and the embattled man to face the disruption of trust, compassion and loyalty implicit in the bond of 'father, friend, comrade.' Following Mutulu's incarceration, this private tragedy fanned outward.

Shakur, Shakur, Shakur, Shakur. Said aloud, the name suggests a litany of cultural ambition, the coming together of heroic beliefs in an extended family, a nuclear community. But dispersal and doom broke the circle. Lumumba was found murdered in Louisiana just before Mutulu's arrest. Assata Shakur, the woman most often confused with Afeni in the mainstream media, (she was born Joanne Chesimard) gained prominence in 1973 when she and Zayd Shakur, brother to Mutulu and Lumumba, were stopped by a New Jersey state trooper. In a shoot-out Zayd and Trooper Werner Foerster were killed; Assata was wounded and later convicted. Representing this as an extreme case of Black activism, Federal authorities said Mutulu had helped Assata escape from prison in 1979 when she became aware of a plan to have white prisoners assassinate her. Securing her own legend, Assata fled to Cuba, where she currently lives under asylum granted by Fidel Castro.

The Shakur's tribal activism had become both a legend and a legacy. Journalist Ron Howell reported, 'At age fifteen, Tupac must have been thoroughly convinced that to be a Shakur was to confront the possibility of death at an early age. He was learning such lessons almost before he could walk.'

In the British magazine *The Face*, David Toop reflected on Tupac's upbringing, 'Tupac's family history is convoluted hearsay, but a number of prominent panthers, including Geronimo Pratt and Mutulu Shakur, figured in his early life. Unsurprisingly, Tupac appears to have been torn in half: family connections and his sympathies for the Panthers' revolutionary action on one side; the material world and its pleasure on the other.'

The Source magazine, reporting on one of Tupac's trials, mentioned the support of Attorney Chokwe Lumumba, National Chairman of the Revolutionary New Afrikan People's Organization, acting as Tupac's legal advisor. An ex-Panther, Lumumba took the stand and reportedly testified to Tupac's 'ambition, his productiveness and his desire to be useful to his community.'

Not too many months later, on the night of Tupac's death, Mutulu would muse, 'You pushed so many away. You burnt so many bridges so they wouldn't follow you into battles against the demons you were facing. Knowing well to what lengths you would go. This battlefield of reality is littered with many meaningless casualties.' That's father speaking to son one last time, across a chasm more unbridgeable than the generation gap.

Tupac, a baby of the Black Power movement, wouldn't attain the distance or perspective necessary to critique the ideas he was taught. Instead, he'd be bound to it – ambivalently, of course – through affection. Like Afeni, he would feel the need to achieve some kind of rapproachement with African heritage. All he had was rap's beat to take with him as he bounced on his quest.

During the 1992 filming of John Singleton's movie *Poetic Justice*, Tupac told Veronica Chambers how the world must regard him: 'You've never seen a young Black male grow up, but now you have to watch, and you have to help, because my father is not alive. This system took him, so it's up to everybody else to raise me.' Recounting that in *Esquire Magazine*, Chambers lets the statement stand on its own, supporting Tupac's self-mythologizing. At that time he had not yet been reintroduced to his biological father, Billy Garland. For Chambers, Tupac put on the same act he did for others, fantasizing the incarcerated Lumumba Abdul Shakur as his father. His was a common adolescent fantasy. Like Frankie in Carson McCullers's play on teen isolation and longing, *The Member of the Wedding*, Tupac got a sense of wholeness by projecting on to Lumumba and Afeni as 'the we of me.'

Tupac envied Singleton's stable family. 'John had a father that cared, but I didn't have one,' Tupac told a reporter, who noted his voice became thick with longing as he confessed, 'Singleton knew that part of my pain, because he knew how hard it is to grow up without [a father].' Given the sadness of such an emotional state, hiphop fans and reporters indulge much of Tupac's self-pity without giving it the appropriare respect. When discussing Mutulu's conviction, Tupac told a hiphop convention, 'I know a warrior, y'all, you don't take no bullshit, no crying about my mama couldn't, my daddy didn't stay. He stood up for his own self.' That speech won over a crowd thrilled to see a young Black man take responsibility for his acts. It contradicted the lost-father sentiment that has become a hoary hiphop cliché.

In 'Wordz of Wisdom,' Tupac buckjumped over his

depression in order to achieve communion with the people and beliefs that he felt were his inheritance. This search is also apparent in the musical track of 'Wordz of Wisdom.' It is laid-back yet steady, depicting a subtle assertiveness.

'Wordz of Wisdom' also displays an artistic and political inheritance. Gil Scott-Heron would be part of the cultural indoctrination that was mother's milk to Tupac's generation. Scott-Heron's knack for polemical poetry, recited to a jazz-funk fusion band, struck an ideological chord. It represented a new gesture of relevance that young folks could groove to and call their own style – a presentiment of rap's own relevant reclamation of the beat. Think of Scott-Heron's music as a parallel soundtrack to the fantasies being ground out in Blaxploitation movies; this was the seventies' enlightened young Blacks' preferred soundtrack. Scott-Heron's new style charted the changes in progressive Black rhetoric in the very cover art of his 1975 release, *The First Minute of a New Day*, that renders the famous Huey Newton pose in the wicker fan chair as a cartoon with a gorilla in the seat. (George Clinton would later parody the pose to more popular acclaim but less political meaning on *Uncle Jam Wants You*.) A lite-funk groove, the track 'Guerrilla' suggested a becalmed revolution – pop resistance through only the most sedate body emphasis. Decidedly unradical – except perhaps to the seventies moral majority blowhards – Scott-Heron was a middlebrow taste that yet struck every brow – even of depressed radicals like Mutulu who must have recognized that at least this wasn't escapist okey-doke. According to Tupac, 'He liked that "Revolution Will Not Be Televised" rap.' Scott-Heron's fusion pushed; its effect came from earnestness more than musicality. 'Trying to get someplace in the human race / 'Cause we need to see black babies smile,' he chants on 'Guerrilla.' And his reference point was to Tupac's generation.

Scott-Heron's seriousness moved listeners with his griot-like doling out of common sense prophecy: 'All the heroes done been killed or sent away / The people know it's winter in America / And ain't nobody fighting / 'Cause nobody knows what to say.' Tupac had been raised during what the title of that Scott-Heron song described as 'Winter in America.' Such Scott-Heron lines as 'America leads the world in shocks . . . the poor go to jail while the rich go to San Clemente' (from 'Pardon Our Analysis') make specific charges, fueling the political indignation that Mutulu would impart to Tupac and forging the backdrop for the indignant feelings one finds in a Tupac lyric. Together, Tupac and Mutulu, who stayed in contact by phone, drew up a 'Code of Thug Life,' listing rules of behavior to discourage gangsta rappers from violence.

The seventies way of analyzing contemporary politics and putting a reaction to it on record is replaced by an internalized disgust with the surrounding world. This is, in particular, a rewind of political consciousness – before even Scott-Heron's generation, where the sources of Black despair cannot be named. While Tupac took passion from his elders, his blind lashing out refuted the intellectual diatribes that characterized the political thrusts of SNCC–Panther–campus upstarts.

This, too, is what is meant by the popular hiphop phrase 'ghetto bastard.' It's a grief that cuts two ways, a feeling of abandonment that swallows up both parent and child. For Mutulu to be locked up out of reach, and Geronimo Pratt, another convicted Black Panther, to be Tupac's godfather but also unavailable for daily counseling, meant shared feelings of oppression and retaliation were still not communicated but lost in each man's bewilderment at the circumstances that tyrannize him. Tupac would admire how succinctly Scarface illustrated it on 'Point of No Return': 'I'm going through / The same shit that my daddy went through / When he was 22 / Now who's / The hell to blame?'

Tupac understood how ghetto bastards feel bereft of cultural guidance because he saw evidence of it all around him – especially in the Bay area's new generation of desperate young Black men. Tupac shook his head for a TV interviewer and wondered, 'I don't know why the message got lost.' It was a typical rap-era statement, referring to how American pop, including hiphop, jumbles messages in a flux of ideas, whether shiny and new or golden oldie. But it's understandable how hiphoppers got sideswiped by the excitement of cultural celebration, fooled into thinking their particular experience is different from their forerunners'. The flattery of Big New Thing promotion can split artists off from their heritage.

Playing this role, Tupac complained to MTV, 'All the society is doin' is leechin' off the ghetto; they use the ghetto for their pain, for their sorrow, for their culture, for their music, for their happiness, for their movies.' That's youthful vanity talking, the force of what has been termed 'ghettocentricity' – a delusion that traps hiphop youth in their own achievements. Tupac was high on media's worship and corruption of Black youth but felt contemptuous of it at the same time. It takes a particular insight to see past this cultural inversion.

After Lou Reed's notorious 1978 'I Wanna be Black' – a racist summation of the white Negro fascination that persists in both bohemian and leftist sympathies – he made a good, underrated album that applied American rock star experience to the adolescent questioning then fashionable in British punk rock. What he came up with, *Growing Up in Public* (1980), stands as a curious rock star document, pertinent to the barely understood maturation process that would become a subconscious issue for which emerging hiphoppers would have to develop inner vision to comprehend. Reed's timely personal assessment of the masculinity he was brutishly taught and that he awkwardly strove toward clarified a psychosocial dilemma that rock – the music of a pampered generation – could not explore well until hiphop grew into that subject almost haphazardly. It was a part of the masculine pressure inherited by young Black men and by Black male artists, through the genealogy of late-seventies songs like 'Papa Was a Rolling Stone' and 'Patches.'

Reed rapped: 'They edify your integrity so they can play on

your fears / And they're gonna do it public / Cuz you're growin' up in public / Growing up in public with your pants down.' Matching the tough street sense of Kurtis Blow's 'The Breaks,' here is the process of commercial exploitation stated directly. Tupac told the media about his similar need to fight for his freedom as a rap performer. He realized, from the example of his elders' frustration and repression, that the industry's access to the public gave him the voice dreamed of for generations, the opportunity to tell the truth, to make a difference. When Reed made an allegory of this circumstance with an updated classical reference – 'Prince Hamlet caught in the middle between reason and instinct / Caught in the middle with his pants down again' – his own pop-professional experience gives Tupac the insight Kurtis Blow was only just coming to.

The Hamlet line is so close to what rappers contend with in the effort to move through life and showbiz with strength and honor that Shakespeare's dramatized mix-up of masculinity and honor has relevance with what preoccupies Black artists in their contemporary struggle for both honor (reason) and independence (instinct). Tupac represents all the Prince Hamlets of hiphop, scions of revolution caught in the middle of industry exploitation and their own political demands. But like Hamlet, haunted by a missing father, and strained, hysterical principles, these princely rappers are often caught with their pants down – showing their ass and exposing the intellectual vulnerability that results from a deep desire to set right long-standing offenses, even if only in the grooves of their own recordings.

Reed's records were among those Tupac was known to listen to slyly, in his private collection and when cruising in his own car. Enjoying the Bay area's polyglot culture and the range of influences gained from his scattered education, Tupac had a whole host of white artists on his playlist: Sinead O'Connor, U2, Culture Club. Lamping among the party-hearty eclecticism of Digital Underground, Tupac took on the nickname Rebel of the Underground. The monicker describes both his individuality and the links he sought between his own experience and hiphop culture on the one hand and his family's political heritage and – equally important – the rest of the world on the other. "Pac got the title "Rebel of the Underground" as a reference to his Panther background, but it also referred to his own way of doing things,' a friend remembered from those first Bay area days. 'We'd be tripping to Neneh Cherry's 'Buffalo Stance' and 'Pac would follow that shit up with some Pet Shop Boys, 'Left to My Own Devices,' and then back that up with 'My Prerogative' by Bobby Brown. Some Bobby Womack shit be in there, too. He was like some kind of underground DJ, doing dope mixes in his head.'

When a journalist brought Cecil Womack and Linda Womack's *Transformation to the House of Zekkariyas* album to Tupac's attention, he enthusiastically shot back, 'That sounds like some dope shit. Where can I hear that!' It's not a rap album, but it exists probably only because of the changed climate in Black cultural thought that hiphop brought about. R&B masters Womack and Womack (brother of Bobby Womack, daughter of Sam Cooke) took advantage of Black pop's new youthful emphasis by encouraging their children to join in the creation and production of the record. They went so far into a personal version of Afro-centricity that they left the pop and hiphop bazaar behind them. Hard-hearted Makaveli could have been rejuvenated by it.

An R&B album evincing the virtues of family togetherness seemed out of sync with the Black self-destruction that fascinated the early-nineties marketplace – even though it might have been recognized as a fortunate consequence of Arrested Development's back-to-their-roots popularity. But these were actually signs of a scrupulous attempt at catching the energy and integrity of the hiphop era – a work of Afro-eccentricity. This doesn't mean simply wearing tribal clothes and spouting Kwanzaa homilies – the guise of many narrow-minded Black folks. *Transformation* peculiarly but sensibly gets in the nap and wrinkle of family life such as Tupac missed.

Perhaps *Transformation* simply stunned the pop industry through its extraordinary, unexpected wisdom. Reviewing their own marriage for the complexities that trouble any mature couple impelled Linda and Cecil Womack to a new consideration of their roots. After visiting Nigeria, they took on the name Zekkariyas 'in honor of their original and true identity.' The transforming act itself is full of faith. *Transformation to the House of Zekkariyas* means to revitalize R&B, if not through innovation, then by confirming its pertinence to (Black) life experience.

The album began with Cecil and Linda, Zekkariyas and Zeriiya, transforming songs composed by their teenage daughters, Zeniya and Zekuumba. It's a family endeavor yet doesn't stray from the Womack and Womack niche where romantic complications provoke lots of feeling and wise reflection. The adult knowledge in these songs goes beyond the scope of teenage girls, and when some of the lyrics strain toward callowness, the maturity of the parents' vocals carries the songs with power and style. The Womacks get past superficial styles and achieve the dream of Family Afro-centricity.

In the period that intervened between the death of the Panthers and Tupac's birth (co-terminous events) and the age of the Black parvenu in Reagan's America, something vague yet momentous altered the parent-to-child, find-your-roots ambition. In the eighties, as the Horatio Alger myth was literalized – deepened – into a tenet of Black social beliefs, the greedily bourgeois *Putney Swope* ideal came to pass. It took many years, many generations of middle-class Blacks struggling to fit in with the typical American plan before waking up and finding a better way. Those years absorbed the fascination with genealogy begun with Alex Haley's *Roots* and then saw that ethnocentricity wane or settle into a more conventional practice of Kwaanza. The Black struggle for a dream would have to overcome the middle-class drive for status and force both family and heritage to come together as a spiritual goal. Afeni tried pulling this off. She had begun by giving her children Afro-centric names that attested to standards of Black independence and heritage that took precedence over notions of propriety held by previous generations that prized Western assimilation. But with Mutulu gone and crack, her East Coast adversary, seeping into the Bay area Black community, she couldn't pull it off by herself.

Recovering from the burned-out pipe dreams of a fallen Bay area, Afeni remained intelligent and articulate. Described as 'one of the most powerful spokespersons' of the activist movement in the late sixties and early seventies, Afeni had faced down the government, she had campaigned for improvement, raised two kids, bounced from ghetto to town to coast. No one who had known her at that time could have guessed that she would fall victim to drugs and all the terrifying things that go with them.

A friend sympathized with Afeni's breakdown: 'Like a lot of women who cope to struggle with a bad situation, I also used. I didn't tell anybody, including my family. I just hid in my little world of drugs.' The intention was to block out the contradiction between drug use and political views. The Bay area had become an arena of waste; its streets and houses, its forgotten history, all exemplified how a lot of people who had once seen liberty in 'the movement' now sought uneasy escape from despair in drugs. 'There were a lot of stressful and disappointing things happening,' former activist Valerie McFall, who had helped organize Jonathan Jackson's Soledad assault, explained. 'A lot of the things we tried to do, we didn't. We failed at it and that's hard to accept.'

In 1990, on tour with Digital Underground, Tupac discovered that Afeni had succumbed to drugs again. 'Here we was kickin' all this shit about the revolution – and we starvin',' Tupac once said. 'That didn't make no sense to me.'

Chapter Five

Children Will Listen

2pacalypse Now, Tupac's debut album, revealed his cultural indebtedness. He was disarmingly impressionable. In retrospect, the sound of Tupac first developing his social view and artistic voice has untold – never realized – promise. Writing and recording this record was his artistic response to the political principles taught by Afeni and Mutulu, Reverend Daughtry and Public Enemy – all his elders who held in common with the Zekkariyases a hopeful parental wisdom expressed in the song 'Children Will Listen': 'How do you say to your child in the night / "Nothing's all black but then nothing's all white?" / How do you say it will all be all right / When you know that it mightn't be true? / What do you do?'

Black parents worry over so much – the correct amounts of carefully weighed morality to dispense against the practical injustices of actual living – and wait to see those lessons heeded. Afeni's need to prepare her child for its own protection, for its own need for revolution, reached deeply into what she believed to be sensible and what she believed to be necessary. For Tupac's guardians, broken and struggling anew, heritage wasn't the certainty it seemed for the Zekkariyases. History bore down upon each of Afeni's lessons and Mutulu's reprimands.

A revolutionary can be shaken to her foundations with this worry: 'What do you leave to your child when you're dead? / Only whatever you put in its head / Things that your mother and father had said that were left to them too . . . ' Written by Stephen Sondheim for the musical *Into the Woods*, 'Children Will Listen' cautions about the lessons inherent in parental instruction – the way children are initiated into ideology, and guided through various mythologies, whether political, psychological or sexual. These mythologies are handed down through folklore – the kind the Zekkariyas parents, in the nineties, knew to make available to their children, inviting them to take part in creating and thus to understand and control.

For young Black families of the seventies, much of that lore was found in the proto-rap expressions of The Last Poets and Gil Scott-Heron. These spiritual fathers took the place of the lost male figures Tupac lamented. Loneliness encouraged his infatuation with a Bad Father – Legs, the drug dealer who introduced Afeni to crack. Misguided Tupac drew from his example of the masculine principle. 'That's where the thug in me came from,' he boasted. At that point in his life, Afeni's entreaties, Mutulu's advice and Scott-Heron 's social warnings had definitely faded. He was going from a one-day revolutionary to a one-man apocalypse. The incarcerated activist-intellectual Sanyika Shakur, who had corresponded with both Tupac and Mike Tyson during their own prison sentences, counseled Tupac about manly competition with other rappers. 'The thing was getting too hostile,' he told Tupac about bad-ass bluffing. Sanyika advised, 'Either he had to smash on his foes or they'd smash him.' But perhaps Sanyika's rhetoric had too many vengeful flourishes to impress the idea of careful, rigorous rebellion. Tupac's boyish enthusiasm – minus the historical reinforcement the Womack kids were privileged to receive – responded only to the cutthroat ethic of the cynical Black street male. Its enlightened counterpart is political prisoners' resentment, not their idealism.

History revealed that Tupac's outlook coarsened rather than clarified. It's Black youth's promise that got broken and the anger in *2pacalypse Now* is intended to represent that. It's Tupac's outspoken response to the mess of modern living. *2pacalypse Now* – well named after the artist's own, audacious sense of social irresponsibility – accurately reflects how kids feel, their simplified sense of political action.

By 1993 much of this was already encoded in wax and Tupac's listening lessons are apparent from the first track, 'Young Black Male,' which samples Ice Cube's 1990 'The Product.' There are references to Public Enemy, whose popularity had already peaked but whose message was still real for Tupac; he built his debut on the political trail PE blazed. So there's delight in hearing hiphop cohere around itself, as though young Blacks were uniting intellectually. But a drawback becomes evident – for all PE's exciting rhetoric and vivid moral dilemmas, the records are lectures not education. KRS-One pompously refers to himself as the teacher but in hiphop that's the folly of the vain leading the blind. What's wanting can be heard in 'America's Nightmare,' a song that confuses PE and KRS-One with actual political activists.

The hiphop generation wants to believe that its defiance has a social value even as it makes them rich. That's a music industry deception. Hearing L. L. Cool J thrive off it on 'I'm Bad' made Tupac one of those hungry children who have not yet developed the moral sensibility to resist.

When Tupac begins 'Young Black Male' repeating the chorus, 'Hard like an erection,' he's basing a social identity on the most basic pride in self. Still at an early stage of self-awareness – the mirror stage – this infant of the revolution can only talk back to himself and the tough talk has no reflection except facile encouragement. Fans related to this and thought Tupac spoke a great truth, but even that response is just the self-congratulation that is built into the record industry's youth marketing. If ghetto kids weren't so desperate for self-esteem, hiphop would never have succeeded as a quasi-political movement. Revolt replaced dancing as a hiphop subject because American society had become so untenable for Black youth that their urge to socialize was, in every sense, thwarted. Neil Young's ode to an aborted fetus, 'Here's one more kid that'll never go to school / Never get to fall in love / Never get to feel cool,' assumes as a teenage right what society has denied to some – what Black youth have had to snatch discourteously.

But this mean living is half-living, half-conscious. *2pacalypse Now* makes a very teenage move by inflating Tupac's ire. There are only a few instances of teenage wit that provide the necessary scale to put kiddie revolution in perspective. Instead, Tupac's invective borrows so liberally from the family heritage of activism that young listeners would be impelled to think a line like 'I don't give a fuck' expresses a soulful righteousness. It's just brash. But Tupac's brashness could be engaging even while questionable. He shared his youthful insolence with MTV: 'I don't want to be fifty years old at a BET We Shall Overcome Achievement Awards. Uh uh, not me. I want when they see me they know every day, when I'm breathin', it's for us to go farther. Every time I speak, I want the truth to come out. Every time I speak I want [them to] shiver, I don't want them to be like they know what I'm gonna say cuz it's [always] polite. They *know* what I'm gonna say? And even if I get in trouble, ain't that what we supposed to do? I'm not sayin' I'm gonna rule the world, or I'm gonna change the world, but I guarantee that I will spark the brain that will change the world and that's our job.'

The white folks at MTV may have swallowed this and were

scared by it; some Blacks swallowed it and are taken by what is really a complicated entertainer/politician shtick. Tupac went on about his job as hitmaker/provocateur: 'It's to spark somebody else [who is] watchin' us. We might not be the ones, but let's not be selfish and because we not go' change the world let's not talk about how we should change it. I don't know how to change it but I know if I keep talkin about how dirty it is out here, somebody's gonna clean it up.'

With all this bluster, Tupac gambles with *2pacalypse Now*'s charm. Hiphop youth can claim the right to voice objection but only a few have earned the right, and even less have found the proper language. Sister Souljah's underappreciated album *360 Degrees of Power* displayed comprehensive political thinking, but she lacked Tupac's star appeal and didn't sell sex as an ideological weapon. 'Wordz of Wisdom' uses protest as a way of feeling cool. The schoolboy of Sam Cooke's 'Wonderful World' turns fashionably bitter in 'Wordz of Wisdom.' The tale of police brutality in 'Trapped' urges, 'Naw, they can't keep the Black man down.' When Tupac says 'I couldn't find a trace of equality / Work me like a slave,' he hits that pit of resentment every boy feels verging on adulthood with holes in his pockets. But when the narrative throws a boyhood fracas into the mix, politics are confused with incivility. Spite isn't a sufficient motivation for social change, yet change isn't Tupac's aim. *2pacalypse Now* is content with wrecking shit. And yet the remorse that Geto Boys articulated from 'Mind Playin' Tricks on Me' on never occurs to Tupac.

He thinks in pop terms, though. Eight producers, including Tupac himself, keep the tracks simple, from metronome beats to appropriating the melody of Stevie Wonder's 'Part Time Lover' for 'Part Time Mutha.' The bass voice he assumes for 'Soulja's Story' is a projection of rebel attitude – a fantasy. And supposedly hard lines lines like 'Mama told me there be days like this but I'm pissed / Cuz it stays like this' are, in fact, a new kind of platitude. Rapping dead-end scenarios to kids looking for a way out, Tupac offers fatalism as a reflex. Sister Souljah didn't resort to that and neither has Chuck D; Ice Cube has learned better, while Willie D, Scarface and Bushwick Bill know even more but none of them has Tupac's knack for the easy one-note concerto. He's smooth; he's cute where Sister Souljah was hectoring. That's how he gets by with the theory on 'Wordz of Wisdom': 'Nigga' is not the nigga we're prone to fear but Nigga means 'Not Ignorant Getting Goals Accomplished.'

For a genuine politician this would be called devious but in pop it's just coy. Tupac means to reverse Black youth's value system – accepting the negative as a positive – but his implicit goal is brutish. No doubt he was mightily impressed by the point of view expressed on N.W.A.'s 1989 album *Straight Out of Compton* – a best-selling statement of the modern young Black male's temper. 'A lot of what I been thinkin' about came alive when I heard "Gangsta, Gangsta" and " – tha Police," ' Tupac had mentioned to a Bay area homey. *2pacalypse Now*'s 'I Don't Give a Fuck' came easily after N.W.A.'s breakthrough. Tupac added fine-tuned variations on that Los Angeles group's severity. The song's title figured in Tupac's key dialogue in the movie *Juice*; he instinctively added it to the screenplay. And his dramatic sense is fully apparent on this track. It opens with a phone call, setting the scene of 'just another day in the life, G' replete with homey communication and anger.

> *How much shit can a nigga take!*
> *I ain't goin' nowhere no how*
> *Folks wanna throw down*
> *Better bring your gun, pal*
> *Cuz this is the day we make 'em pay*
> *Fuck bailin' hay*
> *I'm bailin' straight with a A-K*
> *And even if they shoot me down*
> *There be another nigga*
> *Bigger from the motherfuckin' underground*
> *So step but you better step quick*

Cuz the clock's goin' tick
And I'm sick of the bullshit
You watchin' the makin's of a psychopath
You think you can laugh
Behind the wrath and aftermath?
Who's that behind the trigger?
Who do you figure?
A motherfuckin' nine-inch nigga
Ready to fuck and rip shit up
I've had enough
And I just don't give a fuck

It still doesn't answer the problems Black youth face when trying to make their way through the world, but in the song's finale Tupac pauses his DJ Quik-style syncopation and declares, 'I gotta get my fuck-offs.' He flips the finger to 'the San Francisco police department, the Marin City Sheriff's department, the FBI, CIA, BUSH, Amerika-ka-ka-ka, to all you red-neck prejudiced motherfuckas. Gay, insensitive, little-dicked bastards. Y'all can all kiss my ass and suck my dick and my Uncle Thomas' balls.' 'Fuck-offs' had become a virtual genre of hiphop; a specific variation on the rebellion first heard in British punk rock and made an accepted part of music industry practice. But when Tupac ends 'I Don't Give a Fuck' with a veritable echo – 'punks, punks, punks, punks, punks, punks, punks' – he's using the particular Black American meaning of the word. Its implicit sexism implies a value system that judges manliness as strength. His strategy brings social discomfort closer to personal affront than British punk had dared, further antagonizing even his sympathizers' ears. Rock critics don't know but the homeboys understand.

A big irony catches this new level of impudence. On 'Wordz of Wisdom' Tupac grumbles 'No Malcolm X in my history text / Why's that? / Because he tried to educate and liberate all Blacks / Why is Martin Luther King in my book each week / Cuz he taught all Blacks to get slapped / And turn the other cheek.' For a revolutionary's son to speak such reductions suggests he was given a slanted political education.

No teenager whose ego is salved by Tupac's peevishness knows enough to see the limits. Its cheekiness is too winning, a placebo. As the track fades over a lite-jazz background, Tupac epitomizes the development of this new, pissed-off satisfaction by wishing for 'America's Nightmare' to come true. He casts it with assorted rap artists, Above the Law, Paris, Ice-T, PE then links them to Mutulu Shakur, Assata Shakur, Geronimo Pratt His priorities are scattered, plus his earnestness is all wound up with family favoritism. He doesn't see politics clearly but the song stands as an artifact, a declaration of pop confusion.

Talking about the new sense of camaraderie hiphop gave him, Tupac would tell MTV, 'We are businessmen, we're not animals. It's not like we're gonna see them and rush them. And jump on them if they see us. And they want drama? We're gonna definitely bring it like only Death Row [Records] can bring it'. He promised that his next year in show business would offer: 'Static. It's gonna be static for sure. What the rap audience ain't ready for is a real person. You know what I want to say: a real n-i-g-g-a. I'm comin' out 100 percent real, I ain't compromising anything. Anybody talk about me got problems, you know what I'm sayin'? It's gonna be straight up like I'm a street person. That's how I'm comin' at the whole world – and I'm bein' real about it and I'm gonna grow with my music.'

At an earlier MTV session, Tupac wore a red hood pulled over his head to put his statements into an appropriately thuggish context: 'The music that I make now? My next album? Gonna be better and more slammin', you know what I'm sayin'? But by the same token it's gonna be more potent next year. And I don't want no garbage [coming my way]! Anybody talk about me, anybody dis Digital Underground, they got problems. Cuz we large and we all over the country. Anybody dis us they gonna get stomped.' He's really acting now and the MTV interviewer soaks it all up – a cathode-ray sponge. Riding the hype, Tupac televised a new revolution specifically for MTV and whoever else would listen.

'That word is bond,' he assured the audience – and maybe his ancestors, too. 'Cuz this is money. Cuz anybody try to take away Digital Underground's money as a whole, they got problems. We gonna suffocate 'em.' Hearing this, other teens might salute, but Tupac's radical forefathers, sitting helpless in jail, worried.

On 'Crooked Ass Nigga' Tupac flips ill and snaps the chorus, 'Suddenly I see / Some niggas that I don't like.' It's the origins of a vicious anti-brotherhood that fans like to excuse as 'complicated.' It's easy to pump to a track like this without thinking; the intense rhythms of hiphop insure most rap records a potent groove. So Tupac is always automatically commercial, but the rhythms here don't keep your head ringing unless you invest them with a large amount of subjectivity, grooving to the notion of retaliation. That kind of audience identification is what's behind the frequent praise for 2Pacalypse Now's best-known track, 'Brenda's Got a Baby' – it pleases the hiphop heads who cold-shouldered De La Soul's brilliantly dramatic character studies ('Millie Pulled a Pistol on Santa,' 'My Brother's a Basehead') on De La Soul is Dead.

Tupac begins the song's story, 'Brenda's got a baby but barely got a brain,' then proceeds to tell 'how it effects our whole community.' Eventually this tale of a seduced and abandoned teenage girl blames her for being dumb and giving the ghetto a bad rap. After giving birth, 'She didn't know what to throw away or what to keep.' The only tender verse says, 'She didn't realize how the baby had her eyes.' Pop fans reminded of The Sex Pistols' 'Bodies' will note Tupac replaces political scorn with a simple pathetic portrait of moral impropriety. 'Brenda' is actually less forgiving than 'Crooked Ass Nigga.' Young Tupac's boyishness shows in the moral weight he holds against wayward girls rather than bad boys.

'Part Time Mutha' also makes a mixed indictment: 'Cindy was my dope fiend mother' (perhaps an early peak at Tupac's

Oedipal anger). By using the terms and limits of teenage understanding – rapping intuitively as the child of a teenage mother – Tupac goes right to the heart of his audience's sympathies. So that even his description of Brenda's stupidity ('Didn't have a job / Tried to sell crack / End up gettin' robbed') gets the intended emotional effect. To simply hear this as sympathetic requires moral naïveté, looking past Tupac's hardness. The moaning female chorus on 'Brenda' sounds sentimental which accounts for the record rising to Number Three in the rap charts, but it's as deceptive as the trite melodrama in a Hughes Brothers movie – and they shot the music video for 'Brenda's Got a Baby.'

By this time Tupac had developed Bay area friends and music industry associates like the Hughes Brothers, who, in their own version of neo-Horatio Alger Black culture, began to encourage in him any behavior and attitude that would get him paid. With Albert and Allen Hughes, Tupac approached the hiphop depiction of contemporary Black life as marketable depression. In contrast to the Hughes Brothers' comfortable upbringings on Detroit's middle-class westside and in Pomona, California, Tupac's street background and extreme behavior found another eager audience. The Hughes Brothers, excited by Tupac's willingness to impress, crafted in the Brenda video and others they filmed with Tupac an aesthetic dependent on debased Black circumstances and behavior. This early form of exploitation would not be the basis for a long lasting friendship – Tupac and the Hughes Brothers were destined to become courtroom adversaries. (Producer Michael G. Moye told the special Jim Crow issue of *Movieline* magazine that the movie that changed his life was the Hughes Brothers' *Dead Presidents*: 'We have seen the enemy and it is us.') Tupac's early video efforts were built on the shaky ground of stereotype and jive. While L. L. Cool J, DJ Quik and Public Enemy give *2pacalypse Now* its warmest, wittiest flavor, these other pop inspirations are the first hint that Tupac's youth appeal might also be his undoing.

A Bay area hiphop journalist described the uneasy moments of the first flush of success: 'I remember Tupac best as an elated young man with his first real apartment, a one-bedroom joint in Oakland. It was 1991, and Tupac had just returned from a worldwide (hotel after hotel) tour. Before that, he'd often slept on recording-studio couches and on the floors of various apartments rented by members of Digital Underground.'

A party was in order to celebrate the little bit of money Tupac had from working touring, recording and video shoots. 'Tupac showed us all around, pointing out this knick-knack and that, telling us for how much and from where he purchased his sheets and towels, telling us without telling us of his profound relief at having a place of his own.'

He also had two guns, prominently displayed on the lower tier of the glass-top coffee table. As the party went on, with drinks passed around, 'Tupac picked up one of the guns and turned it around in his hands, inspecting its barrel and trigger, bragging excitedly about its ability to do damage.' There's a familiarity in this remembrance that is common to all people watching another's rise in the social order. It also recalls that Martin Scorsese scene in *Who's That Knocking at My Door?*, scored to the 1958 novelty song 'Rubber Biscuit,' where a tossed-around gun suggests lethal potential. Tupac was showing off to a group of friends 'who had all fed him . . . picked him up from desolate bus stops in the middle of the night, listened to his poems before they were raps, and introduced him to girls.'

But this same group, impressed by Tupac's first steps up the showbiz and social ladder, were setting the stage for the way he would perform for the rest of his life. 'We endured Tupac's big talk and big guns,' the journalist confessed. 'No one said anything. It was a combination of tact and trepidation that made us pretend to sip the gritty liquid and watch as Tupac, gun in hand, began to bounce off the walls of his new kingdom.'

Tupac found glory to be fickle. *2pacalypse Now* had sold over

500,000 copies – qualifying for a gold album from the Recording Industry Asociation of America – but shortly after its release, the past made a claim on Tupac. In Oakland, where the Panthers had begun almost fifteen years earlier in response to police brutality, Tupac made his own attempt to fight back. He filed a $10 million lawsuit against the Oakland police for alleged brutality. He said of the incident, 'I know about this from what my stepfather told me. They fuck with me just on principle.' He fit the image of the Young Black Male he rapped about in *2pacalypse Now*. The future – Hollywood – was claiming him too.

Tupac in 'Juice'

Chapter Six

A Star is Bought

Hollywood was looking for street Blacks. *Juice*, the latest attempt to bring hiphop culture to the big screen, was based on a script by New York playwright Gerard Brown and was to be directed by Ernest Dickerson, the cinematographer on Spike Lee's *Do the Right Thing* and *Mo' Better Blues*. After the box-office success of *New Jack City* in 1989, *Juice* went into production to catch the latest pop wave.

A casting call went out early in 1990 to hire actors who could fit Brown and Dickerson's vision of Harlem Black youth; word went from coast to coast. Money B first tried out for the role of Bishop in *Juice*. As Digital Underground's second rapper, he might fit the producer's search for rap authenticity; Bishop was conceived as the era's quintessential bad boy. Tupac came along on the audition – not to interfere with Money B's plans, but counting on maybe the producers wanting some genuine street Black in a small part or to authenticate the movie's background. Instead, Tupac got the role and his Bishop became the movie's core.

This was to be Tupac's first real chance to act since Baltimore. Now, with actual music industry credentials to supplement his efforts, Tupac's creative interests were coming together. As Bishop, he would be able to vent the restless aggression that was keeping him alive out west whether he was hustling dope for survival or angling for recognition in rap. These activities were themselves forms of acting. 'It's what I gotta do, and I'mo do it good enough keep my Black ass off welfare,' a Bay area acquaintance remembers Tupac saying. This style of justification carries a historical backstory that implies the importance of survival. Tupac's imperative shocked many more laid-back or pragmatic West Coast colleagues. However, Mac Dre, one of the underground rap artists, understood Tupac's zeal: 'For him to be recognized as a player by someone on top of the game gave him encouragement.' And Tupac responded with an alacrity that almost suggested an artificially stimulated jitteriness. In *Juice*, that macho drive would prove to be the speed that thrills.

Yes, Tupac's debut *Juice* glamorizes and encourages violence. By its very means of turning complex contemporary African American life into the kind of movie clichés people are used to seeing (and, therefore, don't give much thought to), *Juice* makes the traps and temptations of ghetto life seem attractive. The eagerness of white commentators to defend the film against claims that it inspires violence in youthful audiences shows their distance from African American youth. Their ignorance about the causes of Black-on-Black violence is just what *Juice* corroborates. The superficial protagonists in *Juice* hypocritically flatter b-boy swagger by linking it up with the familiar hijinks of action movies. *Juice*'s supposed moral lesson is indistinguishable from its fascination with the easily exploitable aspects of Black urban life. *Juice* revels but it offers no revelation.

Only one moment works. It's the casual encounter with a

crime-in-progress that begins as a friendly reunion between neighborhood fellas. 'You want a piece of this?' the perp asks in a tone that clearly defines the terms of camaraderie that exist even within lawless, hostile social situations. That's a pretty original, and these days highly plausible, scenario. Screenwriter Gerard Brown and director Ernest Dickerson show their seriousness by letting the moment's absurdity happen without undue emphasis. Their Black nineties variation on *Mean Streets* must be understood as *Crazy Streets* – an update of Martin Scorsese as well as Piri Thomas.

Juice combines urban subculture and social horror genres through the authentic details common to hiphop. The story of four Harlem young men ensnared in violence has a harder edge than Joseph B. Vasquez's *Hangin' with the Homeboys* and shares the advantage of dramatizing the humanity that gets lost in white media statistics about urban youth. Yet it's just as cliché-ridden. Brown, Dickerson and Vasquez face the problem of making personal experience and personal observation fit into the formats of commercial cinema. Scorsese had the artistic drive (vision) to transcend genre and create *Mean Streets*, a genuinely expressive work that is still the standard by which serious urban rites-of-passage movies must be judged. The makers of *Juice* and *Homeboys* are trying to work safely within the confines of Hollywood's notions about movies for the rap audience and so never go deeper than surface authenticity. That robbery-in-progress scene and many moments in Vasquez's superior *Homeboys* script get overwhelmed by a predictable, conventional approach. *Juice* would have been a really good film if, somehow, it could have taken a cue from Hank Shocklee's score (especially the amazing title track, performed by Eric B and Rakim) and replaced convention with innovation. From *Boyz N the Hood* and *Straight Out of Brooklyn* to *Juice*, none of these films shows the invention, the passion or the intelligence – the art – of the music that serves as their background and/or inspiration.

It's plain that the filmmakers are trying to attract

moviegoers who may not be familiar with the narrative innovations of rap, but doing so falsifies the experience that they're trying to convey. Rap's innovation comes out of language and narrative that had to be reshaped and reconceived to contain the language and ideas of the life it derives from. These movies are carrying that life back to the domain from which rap artists rescued it. Where *Boyz N the Hood* and *Juice* succeed as conventional movie narratives – in moments of mawkish misery, showing young men suffering – they simultaneously fail as original works of art. The implicit politics of making African American ironies into all-American truths are watered down by storylines that don't resonate.

White critics may applaud these films because the tales have been sapped of the energy and nuance – the juice – that are essential to their difference from the white world, but when Black audiences lap up these paltry features, they exhibit a twist on white ignorance. They submit to the very problem the films are about: conventional plots and conventional moralism restrict artists who must describe a new set of experiences and, apparently, a changed moral code.

Juice divides interest among a crew: Q (Omar Epps), an aspiring rap disc jockey; Raheem (Khalil Kain), an unwed father with slick delusions; Steel (Jermaine Hopkins), the babyish, overweight kid; and Bishop (Tupac), the gangster. You already know which of these is the most interesting – and by experience you know that the typical way moviemakers handle the bad guy will give no deep understanding of his character, just the 'excitement' of his acts. Maybe Gerard Brown backed away from identifying and exploring Bishop for fear of making a hero out of him, but the concentration on good boy Q misrepresents the film's real interests. *Juice* means to exploit the notion of corrupt, violent power by showing the weakness felt by young men who don't have it but who desperately want to control their lives.

By reducing the story's tension to a showdown between careerist Q and impulse-killer Bishop, Brown oversimplifies the choices that the ghetto offers. His theatrical simplification is an insult because it reduces moral dilemma to the same old chase scenes, fist fights and gun battles, without any moral or political underpinning. There's not enough subtext in *Juice*, none of the religious or cultural background that made *Mean Streets* specific (and transcendent). Brown and Dickerson have not looked too closely at these characters and this may partly be due to the idea that by spreading out they encompass more of the Black urban experience. That good idea may contain a healthy sense of community but it doesn't excuse the well-acted but insufficient views of family life and police brutality. It may, in fact, be this mass identification that explains the abundant clichés.

When the boys decide to rob a store with no personal motivation (or dramatic preparation), *Juice* seems to be fulfilling TV-news stereotypes. Brown and Dickerson aren't doing the work of showing what the robbery *means*. Even a tense, beautifully hectic fight scene in Steel's living room goes dumb. Bishop jumps up with a startling, ferocious display that is supposed to be unfathomable, yet this kind of lethal behavior has not been credibly linked to the group's general passivity.

Reality and genre are unevenly mixed here. Brown and Dickerson come the closest anyone ever has to examining the puzzle of Black malice. It comes through *Juice*'s hyperbole, but it shouldn't be mystified, like the Robert Johnson legends white critics love. We need hard-minded street sense about this type of guy, but Bishop is a nightmare. And Tupac's star power actually deflects insight in the speech that launched so many nineties Black Hollywood stereotypes: 'I don't give fuck! I don't give a fuck about you. I don't give a fuck about Steel. I don't give a fuck about Raheem, either. I don't give a fuck about myself! Look, I ain't shit and I ain't never gonna be shit and you less of a man than me.'

Tupac's force carries this scene and several others. He's a potent actor who clearly knows within himself the secrets of macho fronting. He champs at the bit when watching *White*

Heat on TV ('That motherfucker took his destiny in his own hands'). But talent and force aren't justifications for ignoring how Bishop's anger pops out of nowhere – its lack of motive (a new pop excuse) is part of its mystery. Bishop's behavior is cut off from reason, suggesting a desperate freedom to young viewers. (And scaring the establishment; Paramount Pictures airbrushed the gun Bishop holds out from the *Juice* ad campaign.)

If any movie has plied male teen mystery carefully, it must be *Rebel Without a Cause*, in which Jim's (James Dean's) sense of freedom was an aspect of his higher sensitivity, his superior expression of love. Tupac makes Bishop spectacular, but the movie doesn't crack him open. (If Joseph Vasquez had had an actor as powerful as Shakur, *Hangin' with the Homeboys* might have been more than just a good try.) *Juice* replaces psychological depth with the hoarist action-movie bits: a dead man's grasping hand; the jolting appearance of an enemy and the proverbial bad aim at close range (this time, at least in an elevator). There's no excuse for the preponderance of clichés in movies like *Juice*. It may not take much to bilk $7.50 from the homeboy audience, but it takes more dedication and imagination to do justice to their lives than Brown and Dickerson (among many others) are providing.

'*Juice* is about four kids and their coming of age,' Tupac told a reporter. 'It's not a hiphop movie. It's a real good movie that happens to have hiphop in it.' He was well aware of the pigeonholing that goes on even within the hiphop industry itself. Once again Tupac saw acting as a way out, a means of transcending the limits others would place on him.

'If *Juice* was made in the sixties it would've depicted whatever was down in the sixties. My character is Roland Bishop, a psychotic, insecure, very violent, very short-tempered individual.' Tupac's assessment is invaluable. It short circuits all the sentimentality that many commentators have attached to Bishop, recognizing that he is a means to articulate the rage of young Black men. Apparently, he was quite capable of approaching the stereotype and aware of how far to take it, aware of what it meant and the possible effect it would have. *Juice* gave Tupac another opportunity to get the news out about how he and other stressed-out Black American males felt.

Hiphop fans bought Tupac's image in *Juice* because they recognized it. Identification with Bishop was part sentiment, then self-affirmation and then, like with rap itself, justification. The soundtrack was replete with the moment's best, hardest hiphop – an exhilarating title track by Eric B and Rakim, a score produced by Public Enemy's Hank Shocklee and even a track from the avant-rap band Son of Bazerk.

When it came time to hype the movie, the Bay area was ready to honor its native hiphop son. Alex Meija, a remixer/producer for radio station KMEL, recalls, 'We put a little event together with 'Pac and Digital Underground and we definitely let people know that this was going to be the movie to beat for the summer. He came through and that's when I was really able to see his star quality. He was like a magnet. Everyone was just astonished that he was there. Mad autographs . . .'

Leila Steinberg also knew the moment had arrived. 'Everyone has their thing that gives them their recognition. I'm talking about that beyond star quality.' Shock G and Money B of Digital Underground also gave it up: 'Watch out for this dude. He's sewing up some stuff he's about to do and he's about to explode.'

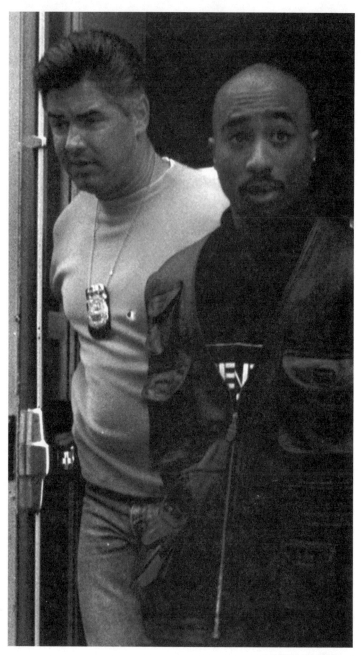

Chapter Seven

Contrasts

Apart from the entertainment pages, it was trouble that first put Tupac's face in the news. Glamor would make it seem to belong there. On August 22, 1992, at a fiftieth anniversary benefit celebration in Marin City, Tupac had a confrontation with a group of street acquaintances – a grudge match that resulted in a six-year-old boy getting shot in the head. The weapon used was traced to Tupac's half-brother, Maurice (Mopreme) Harding who was arrested and released, but the injured boy's family filed a civil suit. This was the worst of several catastrophes that won Tupac his first notoriety.

In Texas that spring nineteen-year-old Ronald Ray Howard shot a Texas trooper claiming *2pacalypse Now*, which was in his car's tapedeck at the time, inspired him. Months later Vice-President Dan Quayle denounced Tupac, urging Interscope Records to pull *2pacalypse Now* from record stores. His soundbite: 'This music has no place in our society.'

Hiphop celebrity was turning Tupac into Public Enemy Number One – with a bullet. In March, 1993, a Hollywood limousine driver accused Tupac of using drugs in the vehicle; a fight followed and Tupac was arrested, but charges were dropped. Less than a month later, in Lansing, Michigan, Tupac was arrested and sentenced to ten days in jail for an altercation in which he swung a baseball bat at a local rapper.

Tupac's profile was as visible in newsprint almost as often as it was in music videos. Hiphop was establishing its own dubious standards for stardom and authenticity, based on the ruffneck image favored in lyrics. Tupacs brought reality and showbiz together when he stormed a Hughes Brothers video shoot with his posse, threatening the twin directors. Reports attributed the dispute to the Hughes Brothers engaging then dismissing Tupac as the lead of the hiphop movie that would be their theatrical debut, *Menace II Society*. Both sides felt the other had gained from their previous collaborations but neither respected that fact or felt obligated by it. *Menace II Society* finally opened in the summer of 1993, the Hughes Brothers themselves became hiphop minutemen, stars of the moment, but Tupac himself had outstripped them and every actor in that movie. Trouble had not only made Tupac's name but also helped make his face recognizable everywhere.

Tupac's second solo album, *Strictly for My N.I.G.G.A.Z* had the effect of imprinting Tupac's image in the daily fantasies of early-nineties hiphoppers. This trained actor and former member of the randy Digital Underground was a minor figure until *Keep Your Head Up*, the video from *Strictly for My N.I.G.G.A.Z.*, became a hit. (The live-wire fascination of seeing Tupac on screen rapping is best matched on the album when Tupac teams up with Ice Cube, Ice-T and Live Squad for cameo raps.) The rapt appeal to women of 'Keep Your Head Up' turned the hiphop roustabout into a Hollywood-style sheikh. (This image would eventually overwhelm even the public alarm at Tupac's coincidental, real-life sexual-battery charge.) Tupac became a star by prescribing romance with respect; telling women to keep their pride, men to mind their bedside manner.

"Keep Your Head Up' is one of hiphop's signal performances. It combines masculine love with social propriety, which is unusual in a form as renegade and disorderly as rap. Tupac's hardness makes the tenderness easy to take – it *seems* unsentimental. Starting with the abused 'darker' sisters as well as the 'sisters on welfare / when don't nobody else care,' Tupac gauges the song to penetrate the personal esteem that is usually denied the Black community's pop listeners. There's a pleading sound in his voice so that he's making a social case for the world to respect Black women, while also plighting his troth to those women who may be listening. This is the kind of troubadour shrewdness that is usually encountered in ballad crooners; Tupac takes verbal seduction back to what was meant by the term 'rapping' when Afeni and Billy Garland and Mutulu were kids. The rap in 'Keep Your Head Up' is strong indeed. Several generations of disrespected women swooned to this entreaty:

Since we all came from a woman
Got our name from a woman
And our name from a woman
I wonder why we take from our women
while we rape our women
Do we hate our women
I think it's time we kill for our women
Time we heal our women
Be real to our women
And if we don't we'll have a race of babies
Who will hate the ladies
That make the babies
And since a man can't make one
He has no right to tell woman when and where to create one
So will the real men get up
I know you're fed up
So keep your head up

Neither Public Enemy's magnificent ode to Black women 'Revolutionary Generation' nor Salt'N Pepa's and En Vogue's 'Whatta Man' had quite the common touch that 'Keep Your Head Up' manages. From Tupac's inspired use of the 'Oooh Child' melody, an emotional touchstone since its release in the seventies, to his steady, courtly appeal, it was the perfect record to redress rap's frequent misogyny. Pop makes these preachments sound like promises; a star like Tupac can make audiences believe it simply by a charming, seductive presence.

And here's the problem: throughout *Strictly for My N.I.G.G.A.Z.*, Tupac, on a hell-raising jag, represents contradictory attitudes, rebutting the communal, feel-good emotions of 'Keep Your Head Up.' On 'Tupac's Theme,' he repeats, 'I was born in this society. There's no way you can expect me to be a perfect person. I'm gonna do what I'm gonna do.' This only reinforces how young the rapper is, how much more of the world there is to experience, learn about and put on the record. Tupac's reckless credo is sincerely at odds with the 'righteousness.'

Strictly for My N.I.G.G.A.Z. complements Tupac's real-life troubles, seeking an artistic, hypothetical response to them. 'I can set the record straight in the studio,' Tupac once told a reporter. That adjustment is clear on 'I Get Around,' a reunion with Digital Underground that describes Tupac's insouciant player attitude. The essence of this track says, 'It's good to be alive.' Sampling Zapp's 'Computer Land,' it portrays the pleasures of bachelorhood and hiphop highlife. A boy's thing, the fun includes money, women and the sharing of both. This is hiphop fancy based in the wild life of celebrity and touring, looking away from its hardships to the ease that one fantasizes about. When Tupac chants in between Shock G and Money B 'loose lips sink ships' his fellatio metaphor also urges that his boys should keep the secret of their fantasy sweet life. The 'round and round we go' chorus at first sounds orgiastic but with repetition hints at exhaustion to come.

But back-to-back with 'I Get Around,' 'Papa'z Song' rebukes the playboy dream with unexpected venom. There's no movement of mind that connects these tunes – it's sheer juxtaposition. Tupac puts all his fears about abandonment, his resentment toward the revolving-door role models and fairweather fakes who churned up his childhood into this song. In 'Couldn't stand UP! / To his own responsibility,' the startled emphasis on 'up' suggests Tupac's discontent with masculine failure, his father's moral impotence.

> *Had to play catch by myself*
> *Once outside a pitiful plight so I pray for a starry night*
> *Please send me a pops before puberty*
> *The things I wouldn't do to see a piece of family unity*
> *Mom's always workin' I barely see her*
> *I'm started to get worried*
> *[That] without a pop I grow to be her*
> *It's a wonder they don't understand kids today*
> *So when I pray*
> *I pray I never grow to be that way*
> *And I hope that he answers me*
> *I heard God don't like ugly*
> *Take a look at my family*

A harried tune, it does as much for ghetto bastards as 'Keep Your Head Up' does for underappreciated women.

It's undeniable that this song divulges troubling auto-biography. The rhyme scheme is slack, the vitriol spewed out rather than constructed. Yet Tupac is able to project an entire generation's woe – a star's gift. In a twist that recalls the bitter vocal shift in the second half of Stevie Wonder's 'Living for the City,' Tupac alters his voice, gives it a horrific, testosterone depth, to portray the excuses made by the absentee parent. A strong voice says weak things.

Maybe it's my fault for being a father and livin' phat
I wanted to make some dough
So you could grow to be strong
It took a little longer than I thought
I slipped and caught and sent to jail by the courts
Now I'm doin' time so I wish you'd understand
All I wanted was
For you to grow up to be a man
I'm so sorry

The guitar picking underneath is poignantly gentle, perhaps too yielding to give the shock that is needed to condemn this common male perfidy as a disgrace suffered by many. Instead it's the sound of breaking down and almost forgiveness. That bellowing father's voice bears an uncomfortable resemblance to the one on *2pacalypse Now*'s 'Soulja's Story,' where the bass notes don't echo distance but vibrate in iron-willed determination. Between these two tracks, Tupac exposes his ambivalence without making a listener conscious of his split – an effort to keep that truth from himself. Somehow the song doesn't grow, or deepen, with more listenings. 'Papa'z Song' is raw, unprocessed. This suggests pain not yet fully understood, a freshly opened wound.

After the shootings and arrests that preceded *Strictly for My N.I.G.G.A.Z.*, Tupac tried to deal with the troubles exploding around him and inside him. Raised to believe in absolutes, he had difficulty comprehending his own ambivalence. He had figured out, 'I know nobody does right all the time but when it comes to the kids and crew, you gotta be there for 'em.' It was a theory based on his own experience, plus his idea of how the imperfect world ought to work. He sought art as the solution: in movies, in videos and most of all in rap.

"I have a group and a program called the Underground Railroad,' Tupac told a reporter. 'I want to strengthen it. The concept behind this is the same concept behind Harriet Tubman, to get my brothers who might be into drug dealing or whatever it is that's illegal or who are disenfranchised by today's society – I want to get them back by turning them on to music. It could be R&B, hiphop or pop, as long as I can get them involved. While I'm doing that, I'm teaching them to find a love for themselves so they can love others and do the same thing we did for them to others.'

This program eventually turned into Thug Life, the short-lived rap group Tupac sponsored. In 1992 Tupac had the acronym he had developed with Mutulu tattooed across his abdomen as a sign of commitment. As the Underground Railroad program evolved into the Thug Life movement, Tupac took in followers across the country, many from the East Coast, including Treach from Naughty by Nature, The Notorious B.I.G. and Randy 'Stretch' Walker, his brother Mopreme, The Rated R, Macadoshis and Big Syke!, a rapper from Inglewood, New Jersey. Big Syke! recalls: 'He was no different from anybody else. Me and Tupac hit it off. I was like "Oh, man, he's a little nut! This nigga's a little nut!" And that's what I loved about him. He ain't gon' back down, he might overtalk sometimes, but little homeys do that. It was the same shit that all of us do. But he was in front of the world doing it. That's the only thing separating him from any other Black young God running around in these neighborhoods. He had the opportunity.'

Big Syke! claims to have wised Tupac up about street life, while Tupac hooked him up careerwise. 'See, if you listen to 'Pac's music, before he got to Thug Life, it was more of a panther-type thought. When he got to Thug Life, it was like, this is where the street, the thugs, the gangstas, the crack, all this [was].' Big Syke! says the group's album, *Thug Life Vol. I*, was tamed by the record company: 'They had watered it down so much, it wasn't even half of what it was when it first started.' Still, it carried Tupac's creativity along. Even Big Syke! was impressed: 'He loved doing music, man! He would just do it like that. He'll write a song in like fifteen, twenty minutes.' Tupac wrote and recorded with an urgent need to express himself. He encouraged Big Syke! to release himself through rap, as he did. 'After my homeboy Big Cato that was like my brother got killed, we went straight to the studio, he was like "Nigga take your pain out on this song." That's what we did and it came out the bomb.'

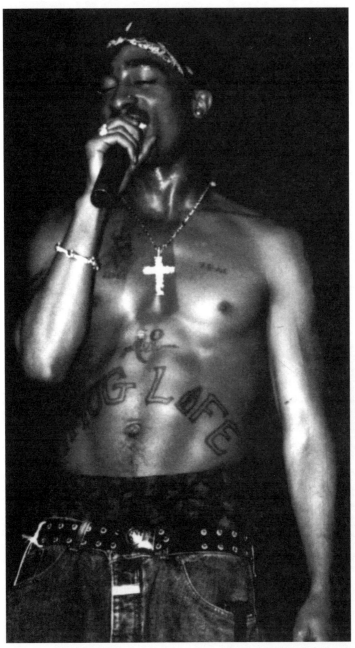

Chapter Eight

Viewing the Body

'Shockingly handsome,' is how *Newsweek* magazine described Shakur when he and Snoop Doggy Dogg had concurrent run-ins with the courts in the fall of 1993. That's an arrogantly racist assessment, yet its twisted assumption about Black physiognomy contains an underlying fear that Black folks – males especially – should not appeal to one's senses but only inspire shock or repulsion.

'Tupac, with his unforgettable big brown eyes and his radiant, natural charm . . .' a male MTV reporter fawned, while reporting how the star waited to be sentenced for threatening video director Allen Hughes.

Tupac had dealt with the pressure of such attention ever since high school. A Baltimore classmate remembered him looking at first abashed at a couple of girls who thrilled at his New York exoticism, then going all out for the admiration. This awareness easily recalls the way a shy teen might react to a group of girls telling him he's 'fine' – he may dress better, brush his teeth more often, and, if at all lucky, he may win the sexual experience – and confidence – to change the very way he walks. He'll appreciate his body's commodity, take care of his instrument.

Such awareness operates deep within the image of teen idols and is intuited in the charm of movie icons who have finessed many levels of the public's adoration. Yet movies have barely romanticized the Black version of this experience. Hollywood shies away from promoting Black romantic actors – it would go against the white supremacy Hollywood was created to endorse. 'They ain't never seen a nigga like me!' Tupac boasted about his advance on Tinsel Town.

While Tupac's rapping endeared him to the core hiphop audience, others, less knowing, concentrated on his rap style. Critic R. J. Smith observed, 'His rapping technique was leaden and hadn't grown much over four records.' What that criticism leaves out is a fact rap fans knew automatically – that Tupac was, above all else, a star – a performer who is good to look at and who embodies recognizable emotions.

That's why his performances on the big screen – in *Juice*, *Poetic Justice*, *Above the Rim*, *Gridlock'd* – and in several of his own music videos are so refreshing. Startling – but not shocking. He commands attention for his ability to hit a precise emotion, plus his wide, dark-rimmed eyes (hooded yet alert) and his wiry sway. Tupac extended that wide tumescent prominence of his nose in the sensual aggression of his *I Get Around* video. The title understated Tupac's wildness while the video used satyriasis as a metaphor for his uncontrollable mischief A star's sexual prerogative and a hoodlum's social threat were combined in one rap icon: Tupac prancing around shirtless, the phrase 'Thug Life' tattooed across his abdomen.

Tough behavior and soft moral sentiments may be part of youthful confusion, but the effect, often, is that the sentiments sound like cant – hollow platitudes. That's why stars cannot be followed as role models; they're often just frontin' – as when

Queen Latifah, to whom Tupac pays tribute on 'Representin'
'93,' raps the hypocritical 'U.N.I.T.Y.' yet still produces
ruffneck, female-bashing artists on her own label. At least Rick
James meant what he sang in 'Super Freak.' Much of this gets
resolved with maturity. Latifah's featured role in the movie *Set
It Off* comes close to a compensation: the film's insulting
fantasy of Black female bankrobbers is interesting only for
Latifah's upfront portrayal of a butch lesbian – a role that made
even hiphop cognoscenti drop their jaws along with their faith
in gossip, when confronted with Latifah's bold feminist
principle.

Similarly, Tupac would complicate his young Black male
image through the sensitivity of his characterization in *Poetic
Justice*. Music video and movies give rappers a physical
authority audio recordings can't match. Tupac's body, even
when put on display, was his area of absolute control.

Tupac's visual, physical presence had become a fact of hiphop
culture by 1993 on the basis of his impact in *Juice* and, most of
all, in his music video *I Get Around*. In *Poetic Justice* Tupac's big
screen appearance amounted to a confirmation of what the
attentive pop audience already knew about him. Female
arousal conveyed the larger pop world's awakening. 'Nice
nose!' Tyra Ferrell moaned in *Poetic Justice* as her character
totaled up the physical attributes of Lucky, the struggling
young postal worker and single father played by Tupac in what
will be remembered as his only lead film role. Ferrell's
exclamation articulated Tupac's appeal – even when he lay 150
pounds, five feet eight inches on the coroner's slab – locating
it largely in his sexual allure. Her enthusiasm, spoken
subjectively, stood out from all the film's other dialogue
because it also accounted for his magnetic pull on audiences.
As she spoke it, public response to Tupac was in the air, his
stardom – the irresistible rise of his renown – was imminent.

Movies, the deluxe part of the pop apparatus, put Tupac's
body on the block. Cinema's exploitative terms seem never to

change, whether glorifying the working-class Irish gall of James Cagney, Dustin Hoffman's urban Jewish tenacity or Al Pacino's dolorous Italian intensity – a star becomes an archetype and an original, as one critic described the young Barbra Streisand. A certain amount of selling is inevitable in this showbiz contract; it can enhance or destroy a performer depending upon his/her ability to cope with lifestyle changes and manage (control) career opportunities. 'I am my own commodity,' Elizabeth Taylor testified before a congressional hearing in the eighties – a memorable statement that contrasts the axiom 'My body is my instrument' of actors seeking an analogy to endow their profession with the craft and esteem associated with musicianship.

By 1993 most pop audiences would have to be aware of the performer/object puzzle. The audience's full appreciation of Tupac's 'qualities' includes an awareness of his possible commercial use – their enjoyment complies with his exploitation. Audiences depend on human display and take pleasure from it, but it may exact an unaccountable, unforeseeable price from the performer who is focused in the world's attention. The stud in Tupac's left nostril suggests he'd been made to take notice of his nose's sleek protuberance and its sensual effect long before Ferrell made mention of it. (That line was either improvised by the actress or customized by screenwriter-director John Singleton to fit Tupac's image.) Such evidence of style is always a sign of self-awareness, proof of an individual's concern with public perception – Afeni herself wore a nose ring, ratifying the ornament for Tupac as an emblem of pride, suitable to adorn an African American prince. The showiness of public performance – as when Tupac and other rappers readily mention the act of recording and touring and being watched – becomes a subject of the songs themselves. Rappers pointedly emphasize their deliberate, showy artistry – they are bejeweled with creativity. Their bodies shine, their records vibrate. The spectacular sense of music as beats, riffs as samples and rhymes as familiar quotations demonstrates a new value accorded to art – and at the same time to human endeavor.

'We were meant to be kept down / Just can't understand why we get respect now,' Tupac rapped against the restraint and disparagement Black artists endure. But hiphop's boastful determination adds a layer of existential complexity to the task. A drummer can pound a beat simply but it carries an echo of historical, sociological connotations. Tupac knew this; it's apparent in the way he borrowed L. L. Cool J and Public Enemy beats on his first album. In the same way the hiphop generations make their own music with subtle or blatant associations with their past, wearing cultural totems like a crown.

Until the proven, lucrative benefits of hiphop, there's no Hollywood image of Black youth anyone can readily put a name to. Earlier showbiz images come from the stage or the record industry – young Sammy Davis Jr, Frankie Lymon, Michael Jackson. It remained for Tupac to embody on screen young Black male tensions and ambitions (following Ice Cube's *Boyz N the Hood* debut) and the assortment of young b-boy dreamboats, nice guys and ruffnecks in music video.

Throwing himself on screen, twenty feet tall, fifty feet wide, as a quicksilver villain or heartaching lover, sparked a new audience response like Ferrell expressed – particularly for many women in the audience but for men also surprised by the masculine efficiency of Tupac's image. The sexual and social potential his body represented had to jolt even Tupac, especially in that proverbial junior-high-school way. It's the existential shock of being recognized by others for abilities – or fantasies – one may not ever have imagined.

Tupac's next step was either to accept his effect on his society or to carefully accommodate what he perceived as its demands. The archetype/original thus follows a style and sets it. That's the story told by Tupac's body art. 'It's my body,' Tupac told a friend about his getting his nose stud. 'And I'm gonna do with it what I want, not what somebody tells me I ought to do with it!' Elaborately tattooed, the rapper made his connection to the fast-growing nineties fad of self-inscription though obviously, by the time Tupac's body took its final bullet, the selective decorations had surpassed the stage of being an accessory. Like the exotic stud in his nose, Tupac's body tattoos signified his objecting to pop conformity. Script and design spread across his flesh, suggesting something like a road map's routes.

Tattoos are communiqués to the cognoscenti – a rose means love, a dagger means danger – none of it means anything true, just what the bearer wishes to be true. 'I'm not gonna explain all these to you,' Tupac snapped at a reporter. 'Read 'em yourself. You can read, can't you!' His tattoos put his inside thoughts outside – the secret me for you to see. Still not really me – just me frustrated, straining to be something or other, something *more* than a skinny mama's boy looking for daddy. Tattoos built of ink and fantasy and paint portrayed Tupac's psyche in certain arch, idealized, enigmatic figures. He traded his own skin for an exoskeleton.

On Tupac's brown, muscled flesh, one can read the same evidence of bewildered desperation that each year peeks out more ghostly in Michael Jackson's emaciated frame. This personal terror is also evident in Prince's recent cosmetic graffito, 'Slave' – a very hiphop notion (along with Prince's gun-shaped microphone), it abuses political history to make a mere corporate point. Prince invokes slavery to deflect from his privilege and to justify his petulance, same as many rappers do. Jackson, Prince and Tupac are related in their internalized confusion about showbiz and racial politics. Sixties soul stars conformed their images – Cooke, Redding, Tex, Pickett, Gaye looked like interchangeable Negroes.

With new chances to speak out one's anger and to have some control over destiny, Black pop stars in the eighties and nineties shunned conformity and curiously reversed the old blackface compulsion. They no longer hide their identities but

choose *outré* identities that hide psychic torment in physical –
often sexual – insignia. Hiphop's earlier, presumably innocent
days, featured Melle Mel of Grandmaster Flash and the
Furious Five taking to leather and chains, emblems of sado-
masochism; Melle Mel flaunted his desire for strength – to
compensate feelings of weakness and oppression. Tupac
similarly chose the S&M markings favored in prisons to make
an affinity with hard-luck brothers. This put 'inside' stress on
the outside – on his body and in the world.

Tupac's markings were doubly meaningful: they created a
tribal code and by the unique methods of primitive tattooing
– prisoners use a cassette motor and guitar string set-up to put
messages in flesh – they indicate music industry indenture.
These elaborate ideograms are intended to make the bearer
exclusive, hardcore and sexy. But tattooing gave Tupac a
costume like any other. His array included:

*THUG LIFE across abs
* *2pac* on right pec
* *50 niggaz* over sternum
* *Nefertifi* over left pec
* *Outlaw* on right forearm
*Christ in flames and crown of thorns on right bicep
*Serpent with jaws open on right shoulder
* *Playaz* on nape of neck
*German cross with Exodus 18:11 across back
* *Laugh Now* with mask of comedy
* *Cry Later* with mask of tragedy on lower sides of back
* *Fuck the World* in script across shoulder blades

This *Modern Primitives* icon that Tupac made of himself is
likely to mean as much to his generation as the famous George
Lois photograph of Muhammad Ali as St Sebastian did for
another. In the nineties, slings and arrows are replaced by
provocative words. (When New York's Whitney Museum
mounted its scandalous *Black Male Show* in 1995, it featured a

photo of Tupac – gun in waistband, scowl on his face, flipping the bird with his right hand – that messed with his wider social stereotype by subtly implicating him in what is actually a gay porn pose.)

Tupac's palimpsest body was as marked by superstitions, traditional beliefs and delirium as Robert DeNiro's as Matthew Cady in *Cape Fear*. Tupac's torso looked the way rap record samples sound. Ideas overlapping, bumping into each other, cultural graffiti blotting out nature, contentment. The same logorrhea crowds the liner notes on his albums:

THANX 2 ALL MY KOMRADZ IN EVERY BOROUGH OF EVERY CITY OF EVERY STATE. THANX TO THE GHETTO STARZ AND FUTURE THUG KINGZ & QUEENZ. MONEY OVER BYTCHES (NOTE: SOME OF U NIGGAZ IZ BYTCHES 2).

THANX 2 ALL THE TRUE MOTHERFUKAZ – THANX 4 BEING DOWN 4 MY COME UP NO NAMES NEEDED

FUCK THE MEDIA! FUCK QUAYLE! THANK THE LORD!

I FINALLY MADE IT OUT OF THE GHETTO, WHO'S NEXT!

FUCK ALL POLICE, SKINHEADS, NAZI WHATEVER! !

As a man thinketh so is his body. Tattooed 'Pac was visual collage, he read as a paroxysm of codes – a walking emblem of our era's philosophical chaos. To get this across was the reason Tupac endured having THUG LIFE written across his abdomen. He was in love with acronyms. From the one in the album cover (N.I.G.G.A.Z. meaning Never Ignorant Getting Goals Accomplished) to the one on his gut (T.H.U.G.L.I.F.E. meaning The Hate U Give Little Infants Fucks Everyone). Rap wasn't enough to convey these messages. Tupac believed in what he could see. He fashioned his own body to be read.

Tupac and Janet Jackson in 'Poetic Justice'

Chapter Nine

Lucky

'The whole world is swingin' from Janet Jackson's bra strap'
— Tupac

Tupac wanted to be a movie star. That's one of the revelations his Bay area manager Leila Steinberg gave to *4080 Magazine*. His ambitions only sharpened after the exposure and reception he got from *Juice* and his music videos. 'He had this incredible, riveting star presence,' video director Marcus Nispel said.

By 1992, a new set of Black film stars, actors and filmmakers were moving into the mainstream. Spike Lee was involved in the final touches of his big-budget biography of Malcolm X starring Denzel Washington. Wesley Snipes, who won notice in Lee's *Mo' Better Blues*, was beginning his action-movie series. Wendell B. Harris won the Grand Prize at the Sundance Film Festival for producing, directing, writing and starring in *Chameleon Street*. And the most celebrated of these was twenty-one-year-old Los Angeles filmmaker John Singleton, whose *Boyz N the Hood* made him the youngest person nominated for a Best Director Academy Award. *Boyz N the Hood* also made a movie star out of rapper Ice Cube – a signal that told Tupac hiphop's time had come. When discussing his career potential he told Afeni, 'Rappers gonna blow up out there!'

And Singleton wanted him. 'When I saw *Juice* Tupac's performances jumped out at me like a tiger. Here was an actor who could portray the ultimate crazy nigga. A brother who could embody the freedom that an "I don't give a fuck" mentality gives a Black man. I thought this was some serious acting.' With *Poetic Justice*, Singleton offered Tupac a role that would stretch the abilities demonstrated in *Juice* as well as put on screen a different portrait of a young urban Black man, as recognizable and affirmative as the character Ice Cube had created in *Boyz N the Hood*. In turn, Tupac's hiphop credibility would lend Singleton the energy and authenticity he needed to keep his films from seeming like traditional Hollywood products. By pairing Tupac with Janet Jackson (in 1991 a major entertainment figure on the basis of two breakthrough, internationally beloved albums, *Control* and *Rhythm Nation*) Singleton hoped to fashion a landmark film full of contemporary energy, glamor and romance. Telling a man–woman love story for the hiphop nation, Singleton wanted Jackson to represent the young Black female experience and Tupac to stand in for all the righteous brothers.

Despite their high hopes, the shooting experience wasn't properly 'respectful' when it came to pairing the raw gangsta upstart with a junior pop diva. 'During the filming of *Poetic Justice*, 'Pac both rebelled and accepted my attitude toward him as director/advisor. This was our dance in life and work,' Singleton rued. 'We'd argue, then make up. Tupac spoke from a position that cannot be totally appreciated unless you understand the pathos of being a nigga, a displaced African soul, full of power, pain and passion, with no focus or direction for all that energy except his art.'

Lucky

After production wrapped on *Poetic Justice*, Tupac confirmed rumors that he was asked to take an AIDS test: 'It's absolutely true. I don't know if it was Janet that it came from. But I know that they suddenly out of the blue they wanted me to take an AIDS test for this love scene. I didn't disagree if we were really gonna make love. I said if I can make love with Janet Jackson I take four AIDS tests. But if I'm gonna do a love scene with her just like somebody else did – and they didn't take a test! Then I'm not takin' the test. Not only am I not takin' a test, but get out of my trailer. I was like ...! And they sent like four different people to ask me. First they sent the producer, then they sent the black dude, then they sent John, then they sent the girl. It don't matter who you send I'm not takin' one. It's just to me it's an insult to ask me that.'

Problems went still deeper in Tupac's account of Jackson changing her phone number to avoid him: 'It probably wasn't intentional; everybody changes their number. I mean it was so ... I really thought I made a friend, I thought, "I know Janet Jackson for life!" You know soon as the movie was over it was like hmm, "This number has been changed." And it was like a movie. I mean, it [happened] the day after the movie wrapped. The last day I saw her I saw her and Rene [Elizondo], her boyfriend, I said, "You wanna go play paint guns? We play paint guns, all right? I'm gonna call you. All right?" "This number has been changed." I said, "Wow, so OK, so it was an act." Naw, but I think that's just ... whatever.'

By the time *Poetic Justice* was released, the most one could say for it was that it wasn't that bad. At the very least, it positioned Tupac in the spotlight his fans knew he deserved. Singleton exhibited his fondness for the politics that influence Black people's lives. Why else would he name his romantic couple Justice and Lucky? But, as it turns out, *Poetic Justice* is simply too forthright, too artless and too confused to consciously employ political symbolism.

Singleton takes the subject of female–male relationships

literally by poising Justice a South Central Los Angeles hairdresser (played by Janet Jackson), with Lucky a young postal employee (Tupac) as representations of the best, most striving impulses of young Black people today. A perfect Hollywood romance, like Vincente Minnelli's *The Clock* (1945), worked as a quotidian fantasy, but *Poetic Justice* observes the common details of modern dating. Justice and Lucky spar with each other at first, unable to bridge the ordinary distances between women and men that, today, are exacerbated by the social conditions and cultural stereotypes that make them wary of each other.

In the movie's best if hokiest moment, Justice, Lucky and another bickering couple Iesha and Chicago (played by Regina King and Joe Torrey), stop off at a beach but stay physically apart from each other. Through interior monologues, they express their isolated, bored, anxious thoughts. It recalls the great beach scene in Michelangelo Antonioni's *Le Amiche* (1975) – but without Antonioni's profound sense that the characters are inhabiting a singular moment in time or are going through one of life's many, unassuming turning points.

This separation is Singleton's central metaphor: *Poetic Justice* is about love in the time of deprivation. Justice meets Lucky while in mourning for her boyfriend Markell (played by Q-Tip), who was killed – significantly – at a drive-in movie (a place for escapism where there is no escape). Lucky's emotional barrier is his fouled-up parenthood (he has a daughter by a junkie) and career frustrations (he wants to be a rap artist – Singleton's foolish attempt to make rappers seem like ordinary people). These are not people who have nothing else to do but fall in love; they're desperate for the meager happiness that movie fantasy says is everyone's due.

The success of the mediocre *Boyz N the Hood* proves that Singleton has a knack and the casting of Tupac gives his picture a special advantage. His ability to convey the banal yet meaningful emotions that Black people identify even within stereotypes is as uncanny as Peter Bogdanovich's gift for showing the way people reach beyond their loneliness in superb films like *The Last Picture Show* (1971) and *Texasville*. *Poetic Justice* has two Bogdanovich-worthy moments: the ominous phone call Roger Guenver Smith receives in the beauty shop where he works alongside Justice and the sassy-cynical proprietor (Tyra Ferrell); and the final look of stupefied good fortune that crosses Tupac's face. These scenes are vivid and evocative – scenes that build a mythology whether or not the artist who makes them shows any depth or finesse.

Poetic Justice fails at its most obvious ambitions. The bad versifying – intended to illustrate Black women's unarticulated thoughts and emotions – doesn't stand up to the wit, incisiveness or profane truth of rap lyrics. Justice and Lucky's road trip from Los Angeles to Oakland should inspire a hiphop epic in the classical sense of the term, but Justice seems as dense as Singleton in her failure to reflect on her experiences and transform them into the kind of art that satisfies her intelligence (and enlightens the audience).

At best, Justice is a naïve artist; and this is also true of Singleton, who fills out the road trip with an Afro-centric carnival, a family reunion picnic. Instead of revealing more about the social and spiritual conditions of modern America – as done in the great seventies road movies like *The Sugarland Express* (1974) and *Rafferty and the Gold Dust Twins* (1975), Singleton sticks to hiphop homilies and two-bit ironies. Compared to a great rap record like DJ Quik's 'Jus Lyke Compton,' an aural road movie contemplating the Black ways of life across the country, *Poetic Justice* didn't cut it.

Somehow Singleton made the mistake of forcing Janet Jackson into faking urban toughness when a better film might have been made of a clash between her dainty, princessy sexiness running up against Tupac Shakur's bugged-out ruffneck. As it turned out in 1993, Tupac's friends-turned-nemesis the Hughes Brothers stole Singleton's thunder with their sensationalistic *Menace II Society*. *Poetic Justice* flopped at the box office and later at video rental counters. Singleton had proved himself capable of as wide a thematic range as Spike Lee – an important point for young Black artists of the hiphop era. But unlike Tupac in his recordings, Singleton's style was hesitant. Tupac's idea of hiphop art was more urgent – getting right to the point.

'Above the Rim'

Chapter Ten

Trials of the Hiphop Famous

'I want to be in a movie that don't fuck around. That proves I can act and show something to people,' Tupac boasted after *Poetic Justice* failed to ignite the 'hood. He may have been speaking out of dissatisfaction that Singleton's movie had been trumped by *Menace II Society*, the story of an LA ghetto hell-raiser named O-Dog – the movie role Tupac wanted. The Hughes Brothers ripped the story of O-Dog (played by Laurenz Tate) right out of *Juice* – 'I don't give a fuck' is also O-Dog's signature line. Tupac's brashness inspires the movie even though he and the Hughes Brothers couldn't come to terms on making the film together.

Relations between the filmmakers and the rapper had deteriorated over phone conversations and business conferences that kept each party at cross-purposes. As happens in hiphop, insults flew like rumors and bad blood filled the air like summer humidity. This friction led to an altercation on the set of a Hughes Brothers music video in Los Angeles that year. Tupac and his boys stormed the set, to confront the Hughes Brothers and to settle the conflicting egos. Witnesses say Tupac, swinging a baseball bat, went after each of the twins, cornering Albert Hughes while Allen Hughes fled. The throw-down wound up in court, but stories of Tupac's rage ran through Hollywood. The only role he could get was brief, playing another dangerous thug – a supporting role – in *Above the Rim*, a movie about basketball and the ghetto. Hoop nightmares.

By the end of the year, when Singleton was preparing production on his next movie, *Higher Learning*, executives at Columbia Pictures forced the young auteur to drop Tupac from the cast. (Ice Cube eventually played the role of an angry college student who inspires others to both protest and study Black history.) Tupac was no longer seen as just a music video or big-screen bad boy. He was for real.

That year, Tupac was hounded by trouble. On October 31, he was arrested in Atlanta for allegedly shooting at two off-duty police officers. Tupac said the incident occurred when he was driving through the city with friends. He swerved, barely missing two white women who were crossing the street – wives of local policemen, brothers Mark and Scott Whitwell. When Tupac and friends exited the car, one of the officers pointed a gun at the group. Gunfire followed argument. This was the kind of action that fuels the Tupac legend. As Alex Meija explains, 'If you get pulled over by the police, you wanna say, "fuck the police." But you know what, there's not a camera there while you're saying it. Here's someone in the limelight so when he goes out there and he says, "Fuck y'all," he's voicing what everyone felt.' Because he felt like firing back, Tupac was arrested by the Atlanta PD, then released on $55,000 bail and the Whitwells later dropped their charges.

But the worst was yet to come, and friends saw it looming. Bay area rapper Richie Rich was in awe: 'See, 'Pac was one of them niggas who was doing it. See, some motherfuckers'll do it, and they ain't gon' act like they doing it . . . 'Pac gon' let you know. He gon' bring the motherfuckin' money with him and the whole nine. A nigga was just real ... he was real flamboyant, ain't nothing wrong with it when you're feelin' good.'

Tupac was pushing boundaries. Even Money B recognized an acceleration of the license to groove that he and Tupac had celebrated in such Digital Underground songs as the New Jack valentine 'Kiss You Back' and the Playboy advisory 'I Get Around.' Money B sorted it out: 'You know when you go to a spot, you meet a chick . . . You be thinking, "Damn, I want some pussy hella bad, I wonder if she gon' give me some pussy?" 'Pac would say, "Are you gonna give me some pussy? Can I get my dick sucked right now? If I can't get my dick sucked right now, no disrespect but you gotta go 'cause I'm gonna be tired in a little while. I gotta go and find somebody to suck my dick." And chicks would be like, "Aw, he ain't shit," but every nigga wanna say that, you know, every girl wanna say that: "Nigga, eat my pussy right now" . . . And that's kinda like how everybody wants to be.'

Back in New York City Tupac demanded his player rights at Nells, a nightclub that was once a hot spot for the Downtown élite who shunned midtown for a Chelsea locale. Not far from the meat-packing district – a crossroads of the bohemia, trash and middle-to-no-class transience – Nell's took on a hiphop clientele as the hoi polloi moved eastward. It was the nightlife version of white flight. Ghetto heaven ruled there on November 14, when a twenty-year-old woman caught Tupac's attention on Nell's dancefloor. As Tupac set the scene, with some cajoling, she performed oral sex on him as they briefly danced. Afterward, their private party moved to Tupac's room at the Parker Meridien Hotel, where sex continued and she left. The next day, she returned to the hotel; excusing themselves from Tupac's entourage, they conversed alone. Next, she claims, Tupac's friends broke into the room and began fondling her. Tupac says he left the room, leaving his boys, who then allegedly raped her.

These allegations would stick. For Tupac, month after month became a trial. He began work on his next album, *Me Against the World* – a title that addressed the lowering clouds, the lowering boom. Between the fall of 1993 and the spring of 1994, courtroom appearances would punctuate Tupac's life on the road. His personal authority was being challenged by law, thus society. The Shakur tribe had been here, of course, but the circumstances were different. The times had changed and so had the defendant. Tupac found himself on trial for incidents stemming from personal privilege rather than the defense of civil rights.

"It's like they comin' to get me for whatever reason they can," he told an engineer while laying down a *Me Against the World* track, finishing it against the ticking clock he heard in his head. It wasn't just official society forcing its hand. Hiphop itself seemed to be turning on Tupac when he appeared in court to answer the Hughes Brothers' battery charge. On March 10, 1994, Tupac began serving time for that assault. By the time his fifteen-day sentence ended, *Above the Rim* had opened. It featured a song, 'Pour a Little Liquor,' that Tupac recorded with his Thug Life group. A memorial tune portraying the ritual of mourning and remembrance that b-boys do to honor lost friends, it was based on Ice Cube's pioneering 'Dead Homiez' but it seemed to also be a metaphor for Tupac's own sense of remorse as trouble kept him from his buddies. In this way he dramatized being missing from action.

Few of Tupac's internal worries – the whirring thoughts of rebellion and prerogative that motivated his bold living and hard-driving raps – ever got on screen. Movies were less successful at revealing Tupac's personality. *Above the Rim* (1994), his third film, was part of that series of movies exploiting the superficial image of Black male youths through the sport of b-ball – a bizarre mini-genre famously typified by *Hoop Dreams* (1994).

Screenwriter Barry Michael Cooper, one of the numerous, fraudulent Black journalists who came to prominence on the heels of hiphop (a former *Village Voice* writer, he wrote cash-in screenplays for *New Jack City* (1994) and *Sugar Hill* (1994)). Cooper parlayed black street pathology into a ticket to the big time. His favorite tricks include burying homoeroticism inside supposed ghetto slang – 'You wanna *bount* me? You lookin' like you wanna *bount* me?' – and furthering Black criminal stereotypes. *Above the Rim* indulges easy image-mongering. Tupac has the role of Birdie, a devilish drug dealer who, in competition with his older, straight-arrow brother (played by the actor Leon), becomes a gang leader and tries to corrupt the hood's good-guy ball players. This part can take Tupac no further in delineating urban male chaos than *Juice* already had.

'I put my heart into making Birdie the evillest, meanest, wacked-out nigga. Cuz people got to know what it's like to have everybody against you and you feel like bein' a killin' motherfucker who bring everybody else down if the shit don't work out right. Cuz his world ain't goin' the way it supposed to.' Those words, said to a journalist while promoting *Above the Rim*, are more to the point of hiphop male anguish than any of the dialogue Birdie actually gets to speak. He is introduced as a cigar-chewing bad boy. His second scene frames him in hell-red lighting – an unintentionally funny version of the Charlie Murphy scenes in *CB4*. Tupac's determination to make an original character is given over to Hollywood's (Cooper's) Black clichés. It's not a new turnabout but now the box-office currency of hiphop endows the film's Hollywood formula with a fake legitimacy on things ghetto. To explain himself, fiendish Birdie trips to his righteous brother (Leon), 'I was in a bodega with Mama's food stamps. The niggas were laughin' at me!' It's weaker than any of the motivations heard on a typical Tupac album rant. So is Birdie's boast about buying his mother 'a split-level duplex, big screen TV, marble floors.'

Tupac gives these lines conviction; he understands the common hiphop era weakness for using creature comforts to measure progress. His passionate social reflexes hook into Cooper's crap. Tupac, along with co-star Marlon Wayans (of the

notorious showbiz clan) and Cooper, share the young comers'
compulsion to channel the complications of their striving into
simple commercial narratives, even when it results in trite
moralizing. The video-exploiters of *Hoop Dreams* didn't do it
any worse. The ending of *Above the Rim*, when Tupac is killed
by Wayans, makes it clear that the death predictions Tupac
favored were based in melodrama at least as much as foresight.
Tupac's Hollywood work used fantasy to reinforce his
undeniable sense of dread.

In November, Tupac was scheduled to stand trial in New York
for the sexual assault at the Parker Meridien – his most serious
drama yet. Undeterred, he continuously wrote raps. He began
filming music videos – an additional creative outlet that was an
extension of his enterprising urge. The Shakur family
dynamism spurred him on. He also contributed vocals and
moral support to friends' recordings. Rapper Little Shawn
asked for his help on a new track. Tupac is remembered
agreeing, 'I'm not letting this trial stop me. I'mo make records,
I'mo make movies *anyway*!'

Entering the dank foyer of Quad Recording Studios on
Seventh Avenue, Tupac walked into the elevator, heading to do
a verse for the Little Shawn session, when muggers attacked.
He was shot five times, $50,000 worth of jewelry was taken off
his person, repeated kicks and stomps were put to his prone
body. The apparent robbery, by two men with guns, left Tupac
for dead. Tupac later insisted it was a set-up stemming from a
rivalry with The Notorious B.I.G., the young East Coast
rapper who had been so interested in Tupac's Thug Life
collective until industry rivalry came between them.

After a three-hour bout of surgery, Tupac made his famous
overnight recovery, insisting on immediate release from the
hospital. He went back to the streets with the entire scenario
of the East Coast–West Coast competition thought out and
strategized. 'Niggaz wanna come down hard this way, I be
ready for they asses. Ain't no time to play no more!' he was

quoted as saying. The shooting and robbery were never resolved, but Tupac moved on with certainty, hanging tough as the Shakur legacy had taught. Wounded, he now felt like a solder, like a battle-scarred veteran with the glory of war in his heart. It was no longer simply a promotional ploy to sell records – the East Coast–West Coast Thang became a personal symbol of many scores Tupac was determined to settle.

In court the next day, bandaged and body-weary but hell-bent, Tupac was acquitted of sodomy and weapons charges but found guilty of sexual abuse. (Tupac's associate Charles Fuller acknowledged having oral sex with the woman but insisted it was consensual.) He was sent to Riker's Island penitentiary, where he faced an eighteen-month to four-and-a-half year sentence. Jail is where the Panther and hiphop legacies do a karmic face-off. Tupac began serving time on Valentine's Day 1995.

MC Hammer, Snoop and Tupac

Chapter Eleven

Word is Bondage

Me Against the World opens with a mock radio news summary of Tupac's recent troubles:

> *At 12:25 a.m. Wednesday Tupac was on his way into a Times Square building to record at an 8th floor studio with another rapper. But in the lobby Tupac was shot several times, including two graze wounds to the head. Tupac's lawyers said the attack appeared to be a set-up.

> *AGAINST DOCTORS' ORDERS TUPAC SHAKUR CHECKED HIMSELF OUT OF THE HOSPITAL LESS THAN 24 HOURS AFTER BEING SHOT FIVE TIMES AT A MANHATTAN RECORDING STUDIO.

> *Tupac Shakur won one clean legal victory this year as he is dismissed of assault charges brought against him that he

allegedly shot at two off-duty Atlanta cops on Halloween last year. The case was dismissed due to insufficient evidence.

*More controversy surrounds Tupac Shakur.

*<u>Meanwhile in Tupac News, at about 6:45 tonight Shakur may have lowered his own chances of surviving the attack by checking himself out of the hospital that probably saved his life.</u>

*TUPAC SHAKUR CHECKED INTO THE METROPOLITAN HOSPITAL YESTERDAY UNDER AN ASSUMED NAME. HIS LAWYERS SAID HE HAD CONNECTIONS BUT COULDN'T SAY WHAT KIND THAT COULD PROVIDE TOP-NOTCH SECURITY FOR THE INJURED RAP STAR.

* *The shooting of Tupac Shakur here in New York City once again underscores the violence that surrounds this man once he shot to superstardom in the world of music and entertainment.*

In self-mythologizing, Tupac recognized the scope of his life and career. After so much courtroom, hospital and big-screen bravado, Tupac's third album hit the street (debuting at Number One on *Billboard*'s pop chart) while he was actually incarcerated. It carried a double message of the 'political prisoner' copping a plea like a caught rat – OK, a distressed child. That's what he was at heart – despite hiphop's macho affectations. Listeners who might otherwise be outraged, or confused, by Tupac talking out of both sides of his neck, instead hear the poignancy in his voice and respond to his rock-bottom vulnerability.

So much sentimentality is etched in *Me Against the World* it resembles a tombstone. In the title track a female backing vocalist (Dramacyde – a surefire touch in the style of Dr Dre) provides the song's formulaic basis. Ghetto cynicism is stated then romanticized in contrasting male/female voices, with Tupac imitating lines made famous on 'Ghetto Bastard' by

Naughty by Nature's Treach: 'I got nothing to lose,' he boasts – but for a professional musician, it's a lie.

Tupac's stance first seduces then insults those brothers who listen to him but never had the benefit of his talents or his opportunities. This could be taken as a sign of pop's rich ability to bypass logic for the emotional connection, yet it is also the basis of Tupac's moral complexity – and his betrayal of both himself and his audience. Atron Gregory, his first producer, had Tupac's complicated image figured out: 'A lot of people would like to say Tupac changed, but most people didn't know him. Plus, they only knew him from 1993 to now. You know, whatever they may say he changed, but they didn't know where he came from or what he was all about. He was always about doing what he had to do to make it to the top of his career.'

When listeners identify with the little bit of sense and humanity in Tupac's raps, their response is reduced to accepting the role he crafted in the studio as an expression of his personal and political turmoil. As sold by the record industry, Tupac's compassion became a form of middlebrow moralizing – a distraction from the balanced thoughts and difficulty of honest, rigorous political living.

On 'So Many Tears' – an R&B lament designed for adolescent hearts – Tupac says, 'I'm having visions of leaving here in a hearse,' just like the rest of us. Yet, it's shrewdly commercial, he's also ripping off Geto Boys' lavish morbid rap tunes. But he leaves out his real-life bad behavior that brings the hearse near, the toughness that would make his macabre verses abrasive and interesting. Yet for anyone who's actually listened to Geto Boys' fearful confessions, this is comparatively trite. Tupac's deviousness continues on the album's next cut when he grovels: 'Even thugs get lonely.' It's not a good enough line to move any but the most simple-minded audiences; they can only relate to the sappy teenage subtext of being misunderstood. Tupac's con is exposed by the song's title, 'Temptations.' It's a hood's wink.

Terrible thing is, when Tupac puts himself on the witness stand you can't trust the appraisal of his own experience. 'Young Niggaz' ought to be autobiographical but, dedicated to kids trying to be gangstas (as if Tupac had taken on the Birdie role in *Above the Rim*), it uses a bogus *Menace II Society*, *Sugar Hill* narrative. Tupac appeals to the cliché rather than the truth, encouraging youth to see themselves as stereotypes, not individuals. The song's list of social disasters is not a political alarm, it's banal. And when Tupac offers advice, 'You could be a fuckin' accountant not a dope dealer; you could be a lawyer,' he gives away a quick-fix alternative that sounds suspiciously close to his own yuppie/jailbird worries. If Tupac is sincere about reform, why does the album end up with 'Outlaw' encouraging eleven-year-old kids to gangbang?

Full of moral inconsistencies, Tupac raps, 'I woke up and screamed "Fuck the world!"' But his curse has no target, no purpose, no wit; it's bullshit. So is 'It Ain't Easy.' Appealing to the myth of himself and Mike Tyson as political heroes without ethical responsibilities, Tupac gives a shout-out to Tyson: 'I'ma hold your hand and holler "THUG LIFE!" . . . It ain't easy being me / Will I see the penitentiary / Or will I stay free?' Sometimes the personal is political, sometimes the personal is self-involved. The only album track that wouldn't make George Jackson, Nelson Mandela, Geronimo Pratt retch is the booty ballad 'Can U Get Away,' featuring Tupac's romanticism and seduction unsullied by pretense.

When Tupac blurts, 'I'm just a young Black man cursed since birth,' on 'Heavy in the Game,' his self-promotion gets completely, obviously wrong. He's made a terrible game out of the pitfalls of racism. The use of gallows 'wisdom' (which the weak-minded have taken to be prophetic) in 'Death Around the Corner' actually shows Tupac to be blessed by the music industry. He's a perfect product of an exploitative/destructive system. No matter how many promote Tupac as a symbol of Black male struggle, the female chorus on 'Heavy in the Game' (voices of mother wit) delivers the mercenary entertainer's true, narcissistic epitaph: 'I don't care what it did to them, [the] game's been good to me.' Tupac leans against a wall on the album cover of *Me Against the World* – a sepia silhouette. It's a glamor shot that transforms his eccentricity into matinée-idol mystery.

After *Me Against the World*, his mounting legal battles began to look like a public performance. More and more frequently his name made it into the news. He was hit by the ricochet effect of pop art when that teen who killed a Texas state trooper claimed *2pacalypse Now* inspired him. "Pac told me to' became the excuse of young men caught in that strange, frustrated limbo between fantasy and reality. Equally roguish politicians picked it up and used it to gain political mileage. Both those reactions scapegoated rap culture – the surface motive for a widening cultural gulf between cops and the unempowered, adults and youth, art and the law.

All this notoriety lifted Tupac out of the mean anonymity of ghetto crime into a celebrity mystique that hiphop culture has codified as 'gangsta.' It wasn't always the establishment press that turned a troubled life into entertainment. Dream hampton, a lowercase pop writer, wrote a Tupac 'journal' for white-owned hiphop magazine *The Source* that traded on egregious trivializations of Tupac's travails. She began her article, 'Hellraiser,' by recounting her dream of a Tupac tantrum: 'There's a purity to Tupac's rage. Yes, he's dangerously emotional, but righteously so. He believes something and is willing to act on it. For him conformity means the death of truth. We plead for him to return to the car but he has already pimped his way into the darkness.'

Ascribing 'Godly quality' to his voice, hampton recalls Tupac jiving with buddies in a recording studio with his 'big beautiful infectious laugh, and all is forgiven.' Her suck-up continues with a report on Tupac's 1994 trial for assaulting the filmmaking twin brothers Allen and Albert Hughes. 'Tupac strolls in twenty minutes [after the Hugheses] with the completed tracks from last night's [recording session] blasting in his headphones.' When a hallway scuffle takes place between Tupac and Allen Hughes, who taunts, 'Aww, you l'il bitch! Put 'em up!' hampton gets off her most imaginative line: 'Tupac's heart asks his ears for a soundcheck. Still, he's not at a loss for words.'

This kind of myth-making turns the courthouse experience into farce. It appeals to the capricious attitude of the hiphop marketplace, inspiring fans to take legal dilemmas lightly. Useless exploitation of rebellion is rebellion for the hell of it, a false bravado is encouraged in place of more sober complications. Hampton perverts the sad dynamic of most inner-city courtroom trials that center around Black intramural crimes and grievances.

Of all the criminal charges against him, Tupac admitted the Hughes Brothers' case was 'the only one I'm really guilty of' – a more honest statement than most of what appears on *Me Against the World*. But hampton twists an absurd justification out of this:

> There's an unspoken law in our community that two Black men should never be in court for battery. They should avoid fighting when possible and when they do it it should be fair and not fatal. Someone loses, someone wins. There may be retaliation. In worst case scenarios it may escalate into full-blown violence and neighborhood wars, but never should it be taken to the police.

This is nonsense. Criminally stupid. By these standards hampton would have to agree to witnesses to Tupac's shooting keeping silent and protecting the killers. Such journalism is a nightmare of cultural propaganda, not a dream. (The thought of hampton, allegedly the niece of slain Black Panther Fred Hampton, raising a kid – and singing him Nas lyrics as lullabies, she revealed in the *Village Voice* – is ghastly. Another generation of chaos is on the way.) Fake journalist, part mountebank, hampton confuses her own fan hysteria (she calls Tupac 'the most beautiful rapper alive') with Black political imperative. Her 'Hellraiser' article cheapens the sad truth of what happens to mis-motivated rebellion. Hampton's misunderstanding of the legal restrictions encountered by Black youth leads her to pretend a shallow appreciation of what has become a common American sorrow in the era of cyclical crime bills aimed at corralling social misfits. To treat Tupac's troubles as entertainment shows a lack of sympathy. It's the worst hiphop myth-making because it's bereft of pity.

Wiser feminine instincts are voiced in YoYo's single 'Letter to the Pen,' where she transforms 'Nuthin' but a G Thang' from its original celebration of ghetto cruelty to a hard-edged expression of a woman's loyalty. In writing to her incarcerated lover, her words of comfort contrast the maddening compulsions, the negative and positive forces, that make life hellish for young Black males. YoYo turns a regular love letter into a defensive weapon. She counters 'the system' (referring to her political-prisoner loved one as 'soldier' – an arguable endearment) but, most significantly, she defies male self-destruction by offering a woman's vote of confidence such as hampton could never dream. 'Letter to the Pen' opens up a story most hiphop songs ignore – knowing a convict personally has become commonplace in modern America. It takes a down sister to speak to the forgotten men of the hiphop era – those who pay the less dramatic, dreadful, wearying price for bangin' and mackin'. This is a challenge to the reckless bravado of superficial male rappers and bogus rap journalists.

Me Against the World works out Tupac's memory of strife through imaginative representations of his recent crises – the November 1993 indictment that he and some associates sodomized a twenty-year-old woman in a Manhattan hotel suite. His comeuppance soon after – suffering five gunshots and robbed of $50,000 in jewelry. All this was followed by his eventual conviction on first-degree sexual abuse. By June 1996 he had pending sentences for probation violations in New York and Los Angeles. And yet it's important to remember, *people love Tupac* – women particularly think of him knowingly and forgivingly, with the kind of devotion matched only by their dedication to Luther Vandross and Michael Jackson. They empathize and feel protectively toward the young man the world is against. All this love centers on one magnificently complicated song.

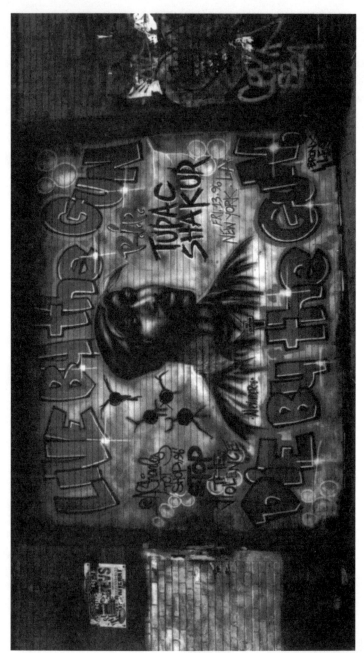

Chapter Twelve

Dear Mama

'Dear Mama,' a tribute to his mother, determined how Tupac would forever be regarded by fans. The main reason *Me Against the World* racked up double-platinum sales, 'Dear Mama' makes hiphop sense because it displays the heart and sensitivity behind a music mostly known for insolence. Tupac may have been serving time for sexual assault on a Black woman, but 'Dear Mama,' like 1993's 'Keep Your Head Up,' made up for it in the minds of his most ardent listeners. If this wasn't atonement, it was still deep feeling – and in the right direction. Where Mike Tyson's rape conviction divided many Black Americans, Tupac's song penetrated even feminists' political defenses through its evocation of a life lived within the grace of a woman's love. Compared to this testament, an infraction with a nightclub skeezer seemed forgivable, indeed.

Both men and women related to the story of family striving and maternal sacrifice Tupac delivered. Slowing his pace to pay proper respect, Tupac made this his most clearly enunciated rap. His memories of growing up seem equally vivid and precise, each detail substantiating the elements of a universal Black American childhood.

You are appreciated.
When I was young
Me and my mama had beefs
17 years old
Kicked out on the streets
Though back at the time
I never thought I'd see her face
Ain't a woman alive
That can take my mama's place
Suspended from school
And scared to go home
I was a fool
With the big boys
Breakin' all the rules
I shared tears with my baby sister
Over the years we was poorer than other little kids
And even though we had different daddies
The same drama
When things went wrong
We blamed Mama
I reminisce on the stress I caused
It was hell
huggin' on my mama from my jail cell
Who thinkin' elementary
Hey I see the penitentiary
One day runnin' from the police
Mama catch me put a whuppin' to my backside

Tupac puts his childhood ignorance alongside his present understanding, placing 'Dear Mama' in the greatest tradition of American folk songs. Yet, because hiphop's revelations are based in social anguish, even the simplest emotions are complicated.

Dear Mama

Put all Afeni's qualities together – Activism, Fondness, Enthusiasm, Neurosis, Independence – and they spell an original kind of motherhood. That's an intimate subject for a young recording artist. In 'Dear Mama' Tupac explored it in the style of those folk songs that touch on a spiritual regard for parenthood and social struggle. This gentle song is, at long last, the answer to the cynicism of 'Smilin' Faces (Sometimes)' that a politically conscious boy owed to the mother who brought him up – and through. 'Dear Mama' is distinguished by personal details reflecting Black social struggle and oppression.

But Tupac's celebration and testimony are not specific to the affection Black children feel for their mothers, nor is it an unusual expression of bad-boy remorse. Merle Haggard got there first with his 1972 classic 'Mama Tried.' It's unlikely that Tupac heard or knew of this white artist, or his country and western song, well enough to append his own version – but the similarities between 'Dear Mama' and 'Mama Tried' are great pop serendipity.

Haggard, from a poor Oklahoma family, spent most of his teenage years in reformatories for petty crimes. 'Mama Tried,' written in 1968, recalls Haggard's imprisonment in San Quentin at the age of nineteen, convicted for armed robbery. The songs are alike in their modes of adoration and repentance. The image and influence of mother prevails over each man's sense of himself, limiting the boastful bullshit quotient almost as though an approving/disproving eye were watching him in the recording studio. Both Tupac and Haggard show what it's like for a rebel to feel humbled. The abashment contradicts the hell-raiser image of both country and hiphop music; it keeps one mindful that the hand that rocks the cradle can rock the conscience of those who rock the world.

But it's the distinctions separating these songs that reveal each performer's personality and the differences separating the cultural traditions and social outlooks they come from. 'Dear Mama' so deeply pierces the heart of Black American sentimentality that a listen to Haggard's version of family love works as a corrective. While Tupac constructs his own sentimental autobiography, basing it on an ode to the woman who raised him, he omits a reality check on the self-indulgent narrator.

> *I hung around with the thugs*
> *And even though they sold drugs*
> *They showed a young brother love*
> *I moved out started really hanging*
> *I needed money of my own*
> *So I started slanging*
> *I ain't guilty*
> *Cuz even though I sell rocks*
> *It feels good puttin' money in your mail box*

This is a remarkable piece of absolution. The ghetto's drug plague (and Tupac's part in it – as a crack dealer in Marin City) is described from the point of desperation *plus* generosity. Swooning to this song involves appreciating its recognition that people sell drugs out of necessity more than meanness. In this view, gangbanging becomes a search for affection rather than a descent into violence. Tupac offers the amnesty needed to those who feel swamped by other peoples' judgments. Indeed, the personal pleading in 'Dear Mama' allows the bad child within every listener to do that popular nineties thing – forgive themselves. It's a short cut to the atonement later sought in the Million Man March; Tupac probably affected just as many people by taking the sentimental path.

Hiphop's tendency to prize passion over cool and cool over truth is an aberration of American pop expression. This happens when an artist acquiesces to the market for Black male error. Willing to exchange tall-tale sentiment for self-examination, a hiphop artist can give in to a romanticism about both his mama and his dreams of freedom that can only lead to confusion.

Haggard avoided this trap because country music has a more candid relationship to its audience.

I turned 21 in prison / Doing life without parole / No one could steer me right but Mama tried / Mama tried / Mama tried to raise me better / But her pleadin' I denied / That leaves only me to blame / Cuz Mama tried

Haggard's mama tried to represent the law to him as an incontestable force – a standard to be respected, obeyed but, above all, loved. You can see the changes in cultural and industry practices in the mama-love song that complements Haggard's, Dolly Parton's 1971 'Coat of Many Colors.' In those days when Parton was a recognizably serious artist (as guileless as Iris DeMent), before committing to the showbiz inflation that sullied her genuine talent and charm, the folk-pop artist's mandate was to speak from the heart, unashamedly, about the virtues of struggle inside poverty. 'Coat of Many Colors' was powerful because the singer's sentimental regard for the handiwork of her mother also exposed the hell of poverty: Parton autobiographically sang of the outside world's (her derisive schoolmates') cruelty. Their ridicule of her impoverished clothing made her suffer the indignities of class, leaving a palpable wound that was so close to the poignance of love the two are mixed unforgettably, almost unforgivably. ('One is only poor / Only if they choose to be.')

Parton's personal politics help explain her determined showbiz climb, but they also represent qualities of integrity that developing folk genres seem to lose over time – and through temperament. Haggard turned Parton's mother love around. While making sense of his own hardships, he created a picture of society more just than Parton's, manfully heaping blame upon himself – an America-first attitude, less insightful than Parton's humanism and the flipside of Tupac's cynicism.

There is something correct in Haggard's self-criticism but it's also somewhat deluded in the way it measures social standards against his own instincts. Hiphop artists do this too, but come up with a different judgment because they know that society's moral standards are, first of all, arbitrary and inequitable.

As Parton's mother represented God's grace and providence, and Tupac's mother the prevailing Black sojourner, Haggard's mother embodied his love for America. In 'Mama Tried' he testifies an ex-con's chastened allegiance. It's not a parole-board hoax; the mama metaphor is there – and it is stirring – because he's sincere.

Haggard's career demonstrates a political alternative to hiphop. 'Mama Tried' is different from 'Dear Mama' not merely because of race or trite urban vs. rural ideas; it's a difference in time and in the effects that history has had on social consciousness, turning indigenous patriots into homegrown cynics. You can best understand this generational difference by considering the changes in American ideology that in the seventies made a patriotic doily-waver out of a Haggard motherfucker and in the nineties turned Tupac, an unrepentant fuck-up, into a mother-lover.

Country and western conservatism has much to do with social complacency ('From a family meek and mild,' 'Mama Tried' begins) and that's what you get in the scoffing, belligerent condemnations of Haggard's 'The Fightin' Side of Me,' 'Workingman Blues' and 'Okie from Muskogee.' Despite the counterculture's espousal of new ways to think about government and morality, conservative artists, rakes and taxpayers reacted with fright and tenacity – a colorfully spoken, culturally authentic stubbornness. You hear the specters of both the Civil Rights Movement and the Vietnam War protests behind Haggard's songs; his jingoism covers up disappointment in the very things his non-political hell-raising protested against. Haggard, like many late-awakening Americans, did not connect his private misery to politics. A callused-over political disaffection readied him for a fight, spurred him against 'petty' laws while traditionally respecting larger rules.

In 'Hungry Eyes,' the underbelly to 'Mama Tried,' Haggard laments 'Mama never had the luxury she wanted / And it wasn't 'cause my Daddy didn't try.' The sense of futility here aches; the patriot who sings those lines must also squirm. Haggard puts longing in the word 'wanted,' but the political key word ''cause' – sung real country – holds an unspoken explanation. With genius Haggard makes ''cause' sound like 'cars' – the American dream of mobility, historically the industrial salvation to much backwoods destitution. The hardship that makes for 'Hungry Eyes' – an image of exquisite deprivation to go with the sad, twangy melody – sounds so rooted it must be a part of culture.

Pure country artists like Haggard resemble rappers in their commitment to a long legacy of desperation: 'Another class of people / Put us somewhere just below.' In 'Hungry Eyes' memory of life in a canvas-covered labor camp shack delineates class conflict without explicitly questioning it. Its terror is in the opening line of 'Mama Tried': 'First thing I remember knowin' / Was a lonesome whistle blowin'' It gives a clear sense of a people isolated by poverty and mired in ignorance, with its attendant mythology of working-class virtue.

Haggard's self-righteousness reveals that he missed out on the good sense of protest that the Civil Rights Movement fomented, not just in Black people but in the conclaves of women, intellectuals, artists, bohemians and gays. It also means that generations later, rappers like Tupac – the ghetto bastards of campus radicals – would have no trouble claiming their right to object to a system of deprivation, to scowl with hungry eyes.

Watching his own mother's suffering, Tupac would pen the most difficult line of 'Dear Mama' without Haggard's social conflict: 'Even though you was a crack fiend, Mama / You still was a Black queen, Mama.' In response to his rock-cocaine-addicted mother, Tupac voiced a sorrier circumstance than Haggard could even imagine.

Rap sophistication includes the awareness of what poverty and social inequity does to people – and speaks out about it more boldly than conservative country and western. And though the reasons for this may also be racial, they derive particularly from contrasting senses of rap's wounded entitlement and country and western's grim forbearance. In the two decades separating 'Mama Tried' from 'Dear Mama,' those polar attitudes have come together – not to produce some ideal country and western rapper (Beck? Aw, heck!), but in the reality of a national, cross-cultural malaise.

Nowhere was this more disturbingly demonstrated than when Afeni Shakur appeared on a network TV interview show to decry Death Row Records' swindling of Tupac's supposed fortune: 'Please remember that my great-grandmother was a slave, my grandmother was a sharecropper, my mother was a factory worker and I was a legal worker. Do you understand? So this represents the first time in our life, in our memory ever, that we have been able to enjoy the American dream, and that's what Tupac brought to his family.'

She echoed the grandmother's speech from *A Raisin in the Sun*, then got down to harsh reality: 'I discovered that Tupac had next to zero, next to nothing. I discovered that the home that he had just bought was not his. Let's say that the entertainment business is a business of prostitution and thievery and that it was rampant around my son. I simply feel that I have a responsibility to my son, whom I carried in my womb, and that has nothing to do with Suge Knight or anyone. That has only to do with Tupac Shakur and Afeni Shakur.'

Facing up to Afeni's qualities, Detroit journalist Emma Lockridge has observed the effects of this tragic spiritual merger: 'I've been haunted by him. Tupac's death to me is the failure of our generation because we're the ones who spawned him. His mother was so full of rage that she finally let this system chew her up and spit her out.' Afeni could initiate and quit social options before her children's own hungry eyes. But her all-too-human travail is reflected in Tupac's contradictions. Unlike Haggard, Tupac witnessed more than his mother's hunger; he saw her faithlessness and her proud Panther spirit broken. His art expresses a deep loss, a greater sense of dislocation than Haggard's rueful banditry. But utter confusion intrudes upon the sentiments of 'Dear Mama' whether or not adulatory listeners choose to hear it.

Tupac could never cover 'Mama Tried' because its sense of trust – its optimism – would seem naïve and totally foreign to him. So 'Dear Mama' gainsays any real sense of Tupac's responsibility, offering instead self-condemnation in favor of her heroism. Perhaps the contradictions of this song represent Tupac's most personal trial, exploiting the most shameless sentimentality in Black pop music. Because of 'Dear Mama,' *Me Against the World* stayed at Number One in the album charts for three weeks, anticipating Mother's Day and until Ice Cube's *Friday* soundtrack rightfully took over the top spot.

'Dear Mama' pours treacle in Black culture's bloodstream and thins the remorse in hiphop ferocity. When Tupac raps about hell in 'Lord Knows,' directing his mawkishness ('If you can make it through the night, there's a better day') to the world of sin and failure and regret, he's asking for pity.

In the melody line of 'Dear Mama' Tupac updates The Spinners' great ode to mothers, 'Sadie.' But the song's basic truth is that mama love lives in Black American culture even past absurdity. It may seem cruel to claim that such affection is ridiculous; certainly Tupac's fans represent a value of loving in their response. But let's be plain. Their emotions confer upon the record a virtue that it doesn't honestly possess.

The extreme 'crack fiend / Black queen' lyric uses the hard truth facilely (even the rhyme is fatuous, building on wack Afro-centricity as the only tribute at hand). Absolution is the secret to the song's success but by ignoring (forgiving) his mother's failure, Tupac always avoids understanding her complexity. He's still looking up, like a child. His best tribute ('You never kept a secret / Always stayed real') is a pretty strong acknowledgment of a parent's commitment to truth yet it wilts when it could have soared by leading to a hard-learned Oedipal or social truth, perhaps detailing Afeni's advice on women, men, revolution. Instead, pathos triumphs.

Tupac and Snoop

Chapter Thirteen

Temptations

In prison Tupac told visitors that when he wanted to achieve something, he would 'find a picture of the thing or draw a picture. Then he would put this picture on the wall over his bed – and he would stare at the picture long and often. He would not sleep in the bed until he had achieved his goal.'

What must he have been thinking those eight months on Riker's Island that turned him impatient and – something he had not been before – ruthless?

Away from the limelight Tupac grew restless and discontent. 'When people tell him how much that record, "Dear Mama,"means to them, he seems to get a charge out of it,' a prison guard told a *New York Post* gossip columnist. Having a hit record in the charts while doing lockdown forced Tupac to examine the effect his career was having on others as well as himself.

Despite a growing sense of desperation that his visitors

could sense, he'd make a goodwill gesture now and then. When one of the guards confessed a family tragedy, Tupac arranged to get the officer tickets to a Stevie Wonder concert, planning with a record company friend to secure the tickets and present them as a surprise gift. But at other times, the odd mix of notoriety and isolation got to him. In Riker's Island's private, steel-enclosed visiting room, Tupac complained to visitors that he was being mistreated, or, when depressed, protested his innocence of the sex assault and expressed anger at the system that now had him 'pinned' just like Mutulu and Assata. A visit from Madonna didn't mean much; the good vibes of a hit single rarely made it past prison security.

Early in his sentence, after 'Dear Mama' had given him cachet as a thug with a good heart, Tupac conferred with Reverend Daughtry, who had made it a mission to pay weekly visits. Tupac wanted advice about his next step – which single to release as a follow-up. 'I felt particularly elated,' Daughtry said. 'He asked me my opinion. He described what the records were about. I then gave him my opinion. That is the decision he made.'

'Temptations,' the next single, was a variation on the sex boast of 'I Get Around,' but as Tupac explained it to Daughtry, he added a veil of piety and contrition to the song's ripe tale of worldly excess.

> *I been stressin' in the spotlight*
> *But the industry's a lot like a crap game*
> *Ain't no time for commitment*
> *I got to go*
> *Can't be with you every minute, miss*
> *Another show*
> *And even though I'm known for my one-night stand*
> *I want to be an honest man*
> *But Temptations on me.*

It was a shrewd move, resurrecting the randy, pre-'Dear Mama' image while inching toward redemption.

Proof that Tupac was held in great esteem by the rap community came with the video *Temptations*. Various hiphop stars appeared in support of the jailed rapper, endorsing in mime the events that had led to his incarceration. Tupac couldn't get out of jail to film a video for the single so they appear in his stead, acting out a drama of mischief along the lines of the frolics that proved his undoing. Black outlawry occurs in nearly every frame so that Tupac's voice-over rap narrates the various ways Black folks get tempted to give in to their lowest instincts. *Temptations* presents these instincts as basically sexual, accepting the racist view that Black instinct – Black sexuality – is innately lowdown. This isn't radical, it reinforces stereotype.

Like a lot of the videos MTV picked up for heavy rotation, *Temptations* showcases Black (mis)behavior for the taste of voyeurs. Voyeurism is also its premise. Ice-T plays a hotel proprietor and Coolio the bellboy who has to make a delivery to one of the guests. While pushing a tray down a hallway, Coolio notices guests conspicuously slipping out of the corridor into their rooms. He peeps through the keyholes and we are privileged to view the obscene:

* *Treach pouring honey on a hottie*
* *Shock G from Digital Underground looking for some*
* *Salt and Spinderella playing strip poke-her (a reference to* TLC's Red Light Special)
* *Crystal Waters with a male stripper*
* *Warren G with money in an attaché case later rolling with a babe in the lucre*
* *Jada Pinkett as an exhibitionist winking at Coolio*
* *Isaac Hayes waiting his turn with her*
* *Bill Bellamy wriggling his toes while getting serviced and videotaping the action*

A seventies pop artist, describing the mystery dance of sex, asked, 'What's the use of looking when you don't know what [it] means?' The same question applies to *Temptations*. A treatise on Black solidarity as well as a pseudo-investigation into the troubles that rise from fornication. Video director Lionel Martin first reminds viewers of the freaky bellboy and hotel from *Barton Fink*, but the 'weirdness' on view (including some bondage and lesbians in a tub) and the evident artifice of performing and spying also recall the hallway sequence in l'Hôtel des Folies-Dramatiques in Jean Cocteau's *The Blood of a Poet*. *Temptations* similarly takes us through the looking glass of Black identity, only to settle for the fetishized images of criminal behavior that belong to outsiders' imagination. Celebrating Black sexuality without social context, the performers mime Tupac's turpitude. Jerry Lewis's 1961 film *Ladies' Man* featured a female dormitory in which a cross-sectional view was to reveal different aspects of masculine ego and desire. Each female resident tested Lewis's constantly evolving manhood. The makers of *Temptations* call up memories of *Ladies' Man*, but their images don't question Tupac's very questionable behavior. Only Ice-T's final dialogue, 'So long, "snack pack," "back pack," "tube sock," whatever,' seems at all satirical. The rest is simple hiphop porn-corn.

Temptations, like other Tupac videos, has more cinematic appeal than his first three movies, yet it panders to the audience and cheapens his pop tragedy, wasting the blood of a rapper. In it, the obscene is seen without understanding – the typical way hiphop remains immature.

Temptations mocks the fact of Tupac's punishment. To think of him in jail recalls a similar image in the *Papa'z Song* video in which Tupac avenges himself on an absentee-now-jailbird father. He gets at a lot of the primal resentments of the hiphop audience. As convoluted as *Temptations* is, it actually celebrates the very same male prerogatives that lead to absentee-jailbird fathers. These are not signs that they or he *overstands* (in Sanyika Shakur's word) the complexity of anyone's only human behavior. Yet young fans who have not sorted through their own complex feelings about present or absent parents, decent or illicit conduct, may feel that Tupac has enhanced their distress. *Papa'z Song*, a convict's star vehicle, is bogusly gratifying, which is the way of hiphop cant. Rap artists seize the kind of truth-telling opportunities previous Black artists could only dream about (from hiphop's prehistory: Sammy Davis Jr's autobiography, *Yes I Can*, gives a good account) only to lose the moment to commercial gimmickry. Tupac's real-life thug life became old news, but these videos stick to the surface of his suffering and the ideals he was searching for. Turning his own precious imperatives into commodities, Tupac was, indeed, playing a crap game.

Paranoia struck deep at Riker's Island. So did confusion. Tupac told Reverend Daughtry that he wanted to marry Jada Pinkett, his friend from Baltimore School of the Arts, seeing wedlock as a relief and distraction from jailhouse horrors. 'He had it all planned,' Daughtry said. 'He wanted me to do the ceremony. The wedding would be in Atlanta.' But in April, Tupac suddenly married Keisha Morris, a longtime girlfriend, in a ceremony at the Clinton Correctional Facility. The marriage was later annulled. As Tupac stewed in his cell, he obsessed on past grievances. In a *Vibe* magazine interview he renounced his Thug Life persona and contemplated positivity. Then in an abrupt turn about, he implicated The Notorious B.I.G., Puffy Combs, Andre Harrell and others in his recording studio ambush.

Jailed fucked with Tupac's head. Play Slick Rick's *Behind Bars* immediately after *Me Against the World* and the difference will seem like graduating from nursery school to the college of hard knocks. No stranger to the docket, Ricky Walters doesn't sentimentalize the tough life that got him into jail; he just pours out the most beautiful wisdom of lessons learned. *Behind Bars* (Slick Rick's third album, the only long-playing rap work recorded entirely within custody – a music industry first) is nothing so banal as an apologia or even a nightmare prison scenario. Rick has done some complicated thinking about the troubles of living in this difficult world. His extraordinary lyrical gifts twist the puzzles, disasters, wonderings together with defiant wit. We risk losing sanity to ignore Rick's contrast to Tupac.

Rick's intricate, speedy delivery, his verbal and literary skills, create a brand-new thrill of thinking from the gut. The title track's refrain ('This type of shit / It happens every day') intensifies rap lingo and poetic expression, making them nearly inseparable: Hold my head and drift / Assume awaitin's knots and cars / Instead of sittin' here accumulatin' / Cuts and scars / Behind bars.' Rick's experience of deprivation, anguish and fear retains its trauma as the song admits his bad behavior and hidden remorse. 'Back in population / Didn't matter that his friends tense / The phone privs, the years added to the sentence / And I escape when I dream / Think so? / I hit the cell because they made a rape attempt.' He zeroes in on the emotional constraints people face, looking outside himself to articulate the unacknowledged suffering of men and women who don't fit the stereotype.

'Behind Bars' carries a listener all the way through the fright of prison to an intricate picture of the way a scandalized mind ticks. Rapping at the speed of thought, Rick exactly conveys how hard-thinking works. 'This type of shit / It happens every day' makes a remarkable chorus, refusing, as it does, a sentimentalization of his troubles. It's a simple but profound awareness Tupac never got to.

During Tupac's incarceration, hiphop went through important ethical and stylistic shifts – changes that created the East–West differences and alienated Tupac, who, for the moment, was no longer actively participating. Locked away, he resented what his nemesis, the Hughes Brothers, did to his family's legacy in their second movie, *Dead Presidents*. 'Those punks are suckers. Suckers. They don't know anything about the movement, about my Auntie (Assata), they just running a game!' he railed. *Dead Presidents* sensationalized the Shakur family's political disillusionment in a flashy, superficial way that made Tupac feel ripped off once again.

Trying to come to grips with the temptations of industry, trying to make sense of the work by other hiphop artists that pleased or irritated him, this was a pivotal moment for Tupac. The Rebel of the Underground, the instigator of Thug Life, faced the Reverend Daughtry each week and heard tell of rap acquaintances putting new moves on the scene. He felt doubt and shame for the ideas that first motivated him. A visitor recalled Tupac's fears about being left out and left behind: 'I need to get out of here and set things up so I can move on these clowns. Rap is stronger now than it ever was, I can't be missin' it. I got something to say to young brothers. Biggie and 'em be blowin' up – and they got wack ideas. I know enough now to go into hiphop with some mad shit.' A friend of Keisha Morris remembered: 'Jail was so bad for him. It got to the point that every time 'Pac heard of some new rap star or picked up on a joint like "Flava in Your Ear" or "Doggy Dogg World" he was wanting to break out.'

Dr. Dre

Chapter Fourteen

In Love With Gangstas

'Is it Dre? Is it Dre? That's what they say everyday in LA'
— 'F – wit Dre Day'

It was time for Tupac to reassess his life. After the all-but-deadly ambush in 1994, he had pulled his physical and mental resources together in a sort of miraculous, myth-making self-resurrection. Acquitted on sodomy and weapons charges, he still faced the guilty conviction and a sentence for sexual abuse. In jail, he had seen his third album climb the sales charts, then watched the world of hiphop spin away from him. New artists were on the rise in 1995, stealing the hiphop moment. Tupac cried 'bullshit' from his jail cell when he first heard people praising Snoop Doggy Dogg and The Notorious B.I.G. But later, he had to admit to Dr Dre, producer of Snoop's hit solo album, 'It's dope.'

The recycled funk of slippery-voiced Snoop and the

extraordinarily adept Dr Dre sounded great to Tupac. The poisonous depiction of ghetto life on *Doggystyle* appealed to a young rap star locked away and deprived of street life, with all its swaggering freedom and empowerment entertained by kids trapped in the hood. *Doggystyle* further refined the formula – already 'perfected' on Dre's *The Chronic* in its gangsta-as-hustler lore. It was a formula that took full advantage of hiphop's growing popularity among mainstream listeners hungry for Black fantasies as a clue to the other America.

Tupac now looked to gangsta rap – LA's Bloods, Crips and Crisis version of hiphop with envious eyes and realized those new beats were hyping up a pop revolution without him. Since N.W.A., Los Angeles rappers had combined social anger, a sense of injustice, with crude, personal appetite. At first Tupac resented the new sound, but he came to crave the wild response it provoked. There was no denying its popularity. And though almost a year would pass before he was out of jail and free to make his own moves, he desperately wanted in.

Revolutionaries compete with pop stars in hiphop's role-model sweepstakes. The lyrics 'Is it Dre? Is it Dre? That's what they say everyday in LA' from Andre Young's second hit single, 'F – wit Dre Day,' were a proclamation of fame, success and acclaim; even in jail it must have struck Tupac as one of the highpoints of contemporary pop, a climax of hiphop possibility. Imperious lyrics rapped to a sinuous groove trumpeted something that Dre made happen – an example of what Tupac himself wanted to achieve.

The simplest dreams of rap success that began with the first bulk sales of Sugarhill Gang's 'Rapper's Delight' in 1979 were hugely confirmed by 1993, the year Dre's album *The Chronic* broke through and changed rap's politics and aesthetics. More money and media attention flowed toward hopeful ghetto talent. A portion of Hollywood excitement, once reserved for movie stars, was now available for status-craving rappers. Dre, an original member of N.W.A., had studied and achieved an expert command of R&B orchestration. A deft rapper as well as an imaginative producer, he had proved himself capable of using a Funkadelic thump and a purely idiosyncratic synthesizer whine to convey new styles of being – of living large in the moment.

Dre's hometown appeal went nationwide. The success that *The Chronic* brought to Death Row Records – the company Dre began with Marion 'Suge' Knight after the split up of N.W.A. – became an emblem of potential that beckoned to Tupac, who now wanted his own 'F – wit 'Pac Day.'

Doggystyle, Snoop's 'solo' debut album – featuring the Dogg Pound and many of the cellmates/artists signed to Death Row – had matched Tupac's previous feat by entering national sales charts in the Number One position – a first for a Black debut artist and an amazing example of hiphop crossover. For all the inside slang and territorial focus used by Dr Dre and Snoop, *Doggystyle* was made with a mainstream American record-buying public in mind. Snoop and Dre had obviously strategized their depictions of hokey street drama ('For All My Niggaz & Bitches,' 'Gin and Juice'), silly, sexist aggression ('Ain't No Fun') and lame acts of violence ('Murder Was the Case') to appeal to the very same audience of thrill-hungry teens as usual. But now it had expanded to include whites and had reconstituted itself as a passive audience of eager, non-thinking consumers. A mainstream critic advised readers to 'buy-play-burn' this 'great record.' But *Doggystyle* isn't a great record and buying it only perpetuates the rotten system it represents. The worst thing about a hiphop crossover act is that it allows listeners from the non-core audience to disregard hiphop's substance.

The lowlife tall tales on *Doggystyle* are lively, vivid examples of Black folks acting wild. Dr Dre ignores how Black folks express themselves in favor of how they destroy themselves. As comical and rhythmic as Dr Dre can make these horror stories – and as cleverly as Snoop can narrate them – the more they allow for escapist displacement of genuine rage. There's nothing on *Doggystyle* that isn't a disgrace to the wonder of hiphop as a politicized pop form made by alert, thinking young people – part of the generation that had inherited some real benefits from the struggle of the sixties. And this is what must have turned Tupac's jailhouse envy into desperation. This regressive rap is for the budded and the stunted – a world of topsy-turvy ethics that paralleled Tupac's jail-cell hell.

Some observers have termed this funkified West Coast illin' as nihilistic. It's actually simpler than that: the wit in Snoop's vocal inflections displays a method of speaking/performing that is fully conscious of the pleasures in dialect and slang. He raps carefully, for the love of speech, for conviviality. Like Dr Dre, with his endless tried-and-true appropriations of the oldest, most familiar P-Funk riffs, Snoop follows the most commercial aspect of hiphop performance. In doing this, rappers may lose touch with the music's protesting value, but they are not nihilistic; they're proudly capitalistic. In contemplating the *Doggystyle* sales phenomenon, the *New York Times* also hopped on the bandwagon, promoting the album even before hearing it. Tupac's line – 'a lot like a crap game' – was vaguely aware of the convergence of hiphop ambition and corporate instinct, two streams merging in a river of greed.

When Tupac, with Reverend Daughtry's approval, chose 'Temptations' as his next release, his unconscious intent was to highlight the slack, stereotyped images the media prefers for Blacks – which made Snoop and Dr Dre the first Black rap stars on the cover of *Rolling Stone*. That image may also go some way to explain why MTV has devoted so much airtime to Death Row videos and rappers' courtroom shenanigans. *Doggystyle* makes humor out of Black deprivation, disguising it as fun. On 'Gz and Hustlas,' Snoop creates a schoolroom fantasy in which he aspires to be a hustler, suggesting that the smart kid chooses crime and gets over. It was a stale routine when Ice Cube tried something like it back on *Amerikkka's Most Wanted* in 1990, but it epitomizes a ghetto myth. Just as Dr Dre's music videos instituted a film genre made up of hitting switches, drinking 40s and acres of dancehall grooving that is now imitated by most rap artists seeking a similar crossover success, 'Gz and Hustlas' distills a version of Black experience that can easily be sold and digested without changing the life or thinking of anyone – Black or white – who hears it. Tupac, newly released from jail, stepped into this void. And though a posthumous *Spin* magazine reference asserts that Tupac 'polarized the races like few pop stars, in death as in life,' this hot new hiphop style offers only an apathetic response to the new realities of social and racial collapse.

Doggystyle's deliberately fashioned West Coast street-life sounds suggest a potential numbness in the mindless beats. Twenty-year-old George Clinton funk riffs, unconnected to a modern sense of agitation, stop being melodic, stop dead in the groove – static. The best hiphop encourages listeners to *move*, but this stuff anesthetizes, pacifies, allows the infiltration of destructive, selfish motives. The romantic descriptions of brutality that Dre and Snoop (and later Tupac) purvey shatter all notions of goodwill and racial unity. This is, actually, anti-funk: it traduces Clinton's spaced-out, feel-good but still political fantasies.

It is not adventurous music. For proof, recall the amazing, booming cellos on Public Enemy's 'Anti-Nigger Machine' (a tune and title worthy of Mingus). The 1990 track not only pushed forward pop music structure but also advanced the possibility of *rejecting* slackness. Rejecting the romance of the gun, Chuck says, 'I never had to be bad / My mama raised me mad' – a line Tupac should have remembered in that it opposes hardness with intelligence, 'mad' being a state of mental preparedness. And behind it all, in that buttery way PE's cello sound expands the vibe, its political message is linked to ineffable sensual pleasure, to love.

The only sign of affection on *Doggystyle* is Snoop's 'Lodi Dodi,' a tribute/cover of Slick Rick's 'La Dee Da Di.' Snoop hooks into Slick Rick's fear and loathing and comical vanity, but he doesn't reveal much of himself, although self-exposure is part of what made 'La Dee Da Di' remarkable. Snoop has bitten Slick Rick's vocal elasticity but he can't dope out his genius, so this version has only shock value, not horror. Slick Rick's confession about all kinds of sexual entrapment seems merely misogynistic when Snoop raps it, whereas the meanness Slick Rick showed to women – with his vocal tricks, veering from testosterone roughness to estrogen squeaks and feigned confidence – opened up a whole world of male insecurity and urban instability to public view.

Black male insecurities are a rash that spreads mange-like throughout *Doggystyle*, even when stylishly rendered by the individualistic Dogg Pound rappers. Snoop plays with this insanity on 'Murder Was the Case,' a poor imitation of Geto Boys' tragic rap theater that knowingly flirts with Snoop's real-life situation as a murder suspect. The remorselessness is rote, but the shameless self-exploitation (something Tupac would emulate) is horrendous. Whom is this song for? Without confronting fear, it lies to the boys in the hood even as it beguiles a crossover audience who may enjoy it and the next track, 'Serial Killa,' as cartoons. Significantly, the cover art of the *Doggystyle* album is a cartoon – a crude imitation of Pedro Bell's ingeniously complex Funkadelic album graphics. Snoop and Dr Dre obviously have no such delusion; they present themselves as cartoons and as fuck-ups to please a paying audience.

When seventies soul group The Dramatics (yes, The Dramatics) are enlisted to provide background harmonies on 'Doggy Dogg World,' it is an unconvincing attempt at legitimizing gangsta stress. Problem is: *Doggystyle* is a long way from the devastating/ecstatic precision and profundity of seventies R&B. The Dramatics just come off sounding as venal as The Dogg Pound, Jimmy Iovine, Dr Dre and the rapper born Calvin Broadus, who identifies himself most often not as a Black man but as a dog.

These aren't the predominant sounds Black folks live by but it's the way a racist social system encourages them to live – and die.

'Why am I so blind? / Why am I so high? / I don't know.' goes an exchange on 'Gz Up, Hoes Down.' It's a cry for help, of course, but no answer or help will come from an audience who is entertained by Snoop's self-immolation, whether they be white slummers or Blacks in the slammer like Tupac.

While Snoop was celebrated by the mainstream, the best hardcore solo rapper of the era was, in fact, The Notorious B.I.G., who displayed the most advanced rapping skills since Slick Rick. Tupac had befriended B.I.G. (Biggie Smalls) in New York, then they fell out over the usual boy–boy squabbles: 'My rap is stronger than yours!' Yet when their personal animosity escalated to intense professional rivalry, Tupac even used the 1996 MTV Awards Show to taunt Biggie with ugly boasts about sexing his wife, singer Faith Evans. As a rap fan, Tupac is remembered saying 'Biggie slams!' But it hurt to be in jail and watch his rivals living larger.

With the release of his debut album, *Ready to Die*, Biggie's bruiser image made him hiphop's equivalent to a Hollywood blockbuster. 'Gimmie the Loot' is an extravaganza that is funnier, scarier, more complicated and more interesting than *Menace II Society*, *Boyz N the Hood*, *Straight Out of Brooklyn*, *Fresh* and most hiphop records put together. No wonder he and Tupac first got along; the rapper on his way to being a movie star surely related to the Brooklyn rapper who was already a star in his heart.

'Gimmie the Loot' jumps. You understand instantly why the album it's from is so popular. Chris Wallace, recording as The Notorious B.I.G., is a rotund young man, big as life. Answering to Biggie Smalls (the nickname teases size with intricacy), he looks like the kind of kid who developed humor and cool as a defense against ridicule. And because he stays alert to the rude, funny ways people speak and behave, you feel alive listening to his record. But since Biggie doesn't go any further than that, his album *Ready to Die* is also enormously problematic.

Playing a subway robber as brash, recognizable and hyped up as James Cagney, Biggie and his partner on 'Gimmie the Loot' trade verses in a hell-raising spree. (A tease, 'I'm a bad, bad boy,' echoes in the background.) Biggie busts the vehemence of young Black criminals who mix up a heritage of oppression and poverty then act out a mean, moral rebellion. 'You ain't gots to explain shit! I been robbin' muthafuckas since the slave ship!' This must be the single most outrageous rap line since Slick Rick's 'La Dee Da Di' and it's so ignorant it resonates. 'Gimme the Loot,' like a thirties gangster movie (or DePalma's more influential 1983 updated *Scarface*), is in the spirit of retribution and impudence; the most desperate youth indulge wickedness (a term consonant with Biggie's West Indian ancestry) to prove, after all, that they are human. Biggie and his boy prey on their own people cuz who else will care? Their social perversion is delineated in a rhyme partially borrowed from Tupac's *Strictly for My N.I.G.G.A.Z.*: 'Big up! Big up! / It's a stick up, stick up / I'm shootin' niggas quicker if you hiccup.'

'Gimme the Loot' trades Public Enemy's cultural solidarity for filthy lucre − it portrays a genuine, lower-depths depravity. Seeing a well-dressed sister, Biggie's stick-up pal squeals, 'Oooh, Biggie, let me jack her! I kick her in the back! Hit her with the gat!' And Biggie answers, 'Chill, Shorty, let me do that.'

This horribly funny track boasts the worst things Black folks can do to each other. Its vicious descriptions of envy and calibrated aggression are also intimately recognizable, easily mistaken for glamor, yet dramatize society's actual 'no hope' desperation which Biggie isn't about to deny. This dread truth, turned jolly and big as life, makes 'Gimme the Loot' an unconscious satire on need turned to greed. Its shoot-out ending isn't tough enough on the ghetto fantasy of power, but the song is closer to being the comic-tragic masterpiece that *The Chronic* was meant to be.

Ready to Die's vision of life is movie-style vivid. It comes from a literalized fantasy upon which the TV generation was weaned. The opening cut sets up a hiphop biography.

There's a clever spin on every cut, illuminating the subjects beyond one-dimensional boasting or simple exposition. The sex track 'One More Chance,' so full of pungent descriptions, is then underscored by '%! ★@ Me (Interlude),' which makes good on Biggie's proclaimed 'stroke of genius' with a hump-and-response dialog structure. It's a parody of sex talk as well as a satire of Black stereotypes:

> *gangsta killin',*
> *chronic smokin',*
> *Oreo cookie eatin',*
> *pickle juice drinkin',*
> *chicken gristle eatin',*
> *biscuit fuckin',*
> *V-8 Juice drinkin',*
> *Slim Fast blendin'*

The humor complicates the track, combining pornography with ethnography – and a good-natured crack at Biggie's physiognomy – becoming art at the end when Biggie, busting his nut and a bedspring, says to his girl, 'I'm sorry.' Flipping the cunnilingus-as-a-sign-of-prowess of 'One More Chance,' he mocks his own male selfishness and clumsiness.

But '%!'★@ Me (Interlude)' is absolutely *not* clumsy. There's intelligence and sophistication in Biggie's self-deprecating honesty. Typical hiphop tropes are used – endorsed – but also tested by absolute charm, artistry and wit. 'Warning' clicks with the right invective, the appropriate, dirty dare (Biggie's 'I get hardcore' is way more fly than the 'get medieval' line in *Pulp Fiction*.) The 'fun' is mistaken for a justified response to dangerous circumstances, as with Dr Dre, Snoop and stupid-acting rappers. This may be ordinary, it may be macho, but it's also childish.

In Love with Gangstas

Call it perspective. That's what separates *Ready to Die* from most other hiphop albums. Biggie's opportunity for living phat could have just caused him to rehash the ghetto stereotypes of *Straight Out of Brooklyn* or even the unmanageable Wu Tang Clan – but there's a richer sensibility here. Biggie's perspective isn't forthright or transcendent like Public Enemy, De La Soul or Arrested Development – it's worldly. Like the best solo rap artists – L. L. Cool J, Scarface, Slick Rick, Ice Cube and sometimes Tupac – Biggie pulls his own weight and views his own course. I don't think his stubborn social sense, his engagement with low-living, is necessarily a truer artistry (he's a serious Biz Markie), but it represents the basic decency of an individual *thinking out* a suppressed culture's isolated politics.

Ready to Die shows Biggie to be fully responsive to the world, but the closest Biggie gets to understanding the world is to reason, 'I rob and steal cuz money got that whip appeal.' The personal disclosure in those lines is recognizable to every rapper and rap fan, you pick up the gist of those lines in every instance of Biggie's and Tupac's bluster: the hurt fuels the yearning; the burning desire obscures a more political focus on how either Biggie or Tupac can achieve what he really needs. Perhaps it was because they shared this longing and this incapacity that they eventually broke ranks – it certainly accounts for their flamboyant presence in hiphop.

The way Puffy Combs's love of voices and Easy Mo Bee's tactile production works, *Ready to Die* reaches out and pinches you. And the pinch feels like a tickle, especially at the end when Biggie blows himself away and the album finishes with aural evidence of life going on (the phone company's mechanical message, a friend's exasperated hanging up). These sounds echo callousness and helplessness but they never quite erase the previous voice of Biggie's very human, very hiphop dejection: this, too, is art.

The album's title, *Ready to Die*, suggests the handy, marketable nihilism that makes Nas's debut album *Illmatic* accomplished yet suspect (it was largely fake, corporate rap).

Yet Biggie, in the inchoate way of street storytellers and neophyte ghetto griots, means something more interesting than being literally ready to die. The obverse of these words is the subtext of the entire album – at this moment, Biggie is *alive*.

Biggie's extravagance – like Tupac's feistiness – was something that fans relate to without the need of a publicity machine. There's a common quality of humor and earnestness related to an ardent involvement with the ideas and language of a culture that makes a rapper big, a genuine folk star, even outside the mainstream's purview.

With success, Tupac tried to maintain a generous sympathy with the hood life he came from. Following Melle Mel's Old School rap, 'I'm a bow-legged brother . . . there'll never be another / I bought a mansion for my mother,' Tupac lived with his mother in a newly purchased San Fernando Valley home that one journalist described as 'a pretty blue-and-white house on a quiet tree-lined street.' But that change in lifestyle actually changed little that really mattered. As much as he craved it, it wasn't always easy for Tupac to contend with fame and success. On the *Poetic Justice* Bay area set, homeys insisted he acknowledge them during a shot. When a journalist pointed out their presence, Tupac answered: 'The young bucks are gonna be jealous. Some older people, too. They got mad because I used to be their gofer. They used to run me to the store. They're sitting there knowing they used to give me money to go to the store and now I've got their whole family taking pictures with me. That's an animosity that nothing I can do can kill, because that's poverty shit and I can understand.'

Given Tupac's empathy it's surprising his jail experience didn't produce a song that takes humorous account of that all-American misadventure. But Tupac wasn't interested in that kind of contemplation. He wanted to be back on top of the rap game, reveling in hiphop's ribald view of the world. Instead, comic rapper Coolio (Artis Ivey) came up with the classic, 'Mama, I'm in Love wit a Gangsta' – a song that opens the rap convict's heart, divulging insecurities Tupac could not.

This song, a duet with female sex rapper LeShaun, conveys the ghetto ethos the way people live it. Like YoYo's 'Letter to the Pen,' the impassioned feminine perspective uncovers a surprising, poignant side. The reality of lockdown isn't just about the imprisonment of lovers, parents or children but the breakdown of social ambitions and cultural expectations.

LeShaun's drowning-in-the-sea-of-love confession can be heard as a sociological report – the news is in her voice: helpless, proud, excited and *unsure*, she conveys the complex emotions of a girl who's gone past innocence. Think of all the genre movies in which women fall for gunslingers and bootleggers yet keep their honor. They could have divulged some of LeShaun's ambivalence but the old forms didn't allow these women to be conscious of their feelings. Brazen LeShaun and clear-eyed Coolio match wits to make a hiphop *Sense and Sensibility*. A woman's personal dilemma gives an acute portrait of our society's manners. Truer to Jane Austen than to Madonna's 'Material Girl' or Whitney Houston's 'The Greatest Love of All,' 'Mama, I'm in Love wit a Gangsta' concentrates on an individual's social engagement, her self-surprising ability to love.

Coolio is so plugged in to life his braids stand up as if electrified. He's sensitive to the *people*, both those who sadly get taken and those desperate to have fun. In his rap sketches someone always pays for ghetto transactions. Coolio gets serious without sarcasm and so the conventional morality dulls the fact of transgression that L.L.'s 'I'm That Type of Guy' made sting. Yet Coolio's ingenuity shows best in the love lyric irony of 'Mama.'

Face it: this woman's song, expressing brother and ghetto love, is something many male rappers wouldn't dare. Coolio and LeShaun represent ruffneck magnetism as an ambisexual thing. The set-up is a young woman's response to her man spending jail time. Going beyond the surface concerns (as seen in Darnell Martin's movie *I Like It Like That*), LeShaun makes sense of her life by describing it:

> *Mama (Mama) I'm in love wit a gangsta*
> *Mama*
> *(Mama) I'm in love wit a gangsta*
> *Mama (Mama) I'm in love wit a gansta*
> *And I know he's a killer*
> *But I love dat nigga*

The echoed 'Mama' is the sound of conscience; LeShaun balks at old morality, yet hesitates like a child before a parent. That's the song's dramatic tension – both Coolio, raging on the phone from the pen, and LeShaun, trying to raise her kids and stay true to their daddy, are straining to fit their emotions into a rough reality. LeShan's 'I love dat nigga' is, in fact, pathetic: love *plus* resignation.

In this love song, affection conveys shock: the truth is, even in debased circumstances people live, people love. There's no pretense; the killer she loves isn't honorable, just a man of his time. 'Mama, I'm in Love wit a Gangsta' is straight up about the guilt and hard work of modern love in which everybody knows/loves somebody who isn't innocent.

This song brings us back to the dilemma Tupac faced in jail, watching, listening and coveting gangsta rap success from inside the house of pain. Revealing young Black men's vulnerability and the devotion of their people on the outside – the song typifies fans' regard for Tupac. It's got to be more than the face and it isn't merely the voice. It's what he stands for as the misunderstood Black male that warms the hearts of listeners who also feel cheated or unappreciated.

If loving Tupac is wrong, his fans reject the propriety of judging men by the standards of an unfair society. They love him for what they feel is the sincere, pure part of themselves and the other fallable-lovable men in their lives. Snoop has only a bit of this, Dr Dre and terror bear Suge Knight have none, but you can bet they recognized it in Tupac's matinée-idol impact.

After he'd been released from jail and signed with Death Row, a reporter observed Shakur fronting for Knight at a Los Angeles food benefit:

> It was Thanksgiving and the gangstas were giving out turkeys in the ghetto. A line snaked down the steps round the side, and along the block of a South Central Los Angeles community center. The free food, paid for by Death Row, was supposed to be doled out at 11 in the morning. The annual event gave Knight a chance to show off Shakur as his latest signing . . . but the pair had yet to show. So the old folks and the moms with babies in their arms waited patiently, staring through the windows at the stacks of frozen turkeys locked inside . . . A couple of hours later the Death Row car arrived . . . having soothed the hungry, Shakur disappeared into the shadow. He might have been the star, but Knight controlled the vibe and Shakur did nothing to undermine it.

That event has chilling echoes of the disastrous early seventies food giveaway that the Symbionese Liberation Army arranged with the Patty Hearst kidnapping – a grotesque iconographic stunt – as well as a lordly potentate bidding that his underlings make him look good. But here, only Tupac remains the icon, despite whatever actual manipulations of power took place. Tupac's welcome into Death Row, the security he felt in hiphop stardom, was a Symbiotic Liberation for Black protest's dysfunctional scion. Even when he was late or bad, his fans felt good vibes. That Thanksgiving reporter also noted, 'Everyone was unbearably polite. "Free Tupac!" people began chanting. Only slowly did another replace it: "Fuck Tupac! Free the turkeys!"'

That emotional range requires genuine affection. The artist formerly known as MC New York had gone west and finally achieved his own 'Fuck with 'Pac Day.'

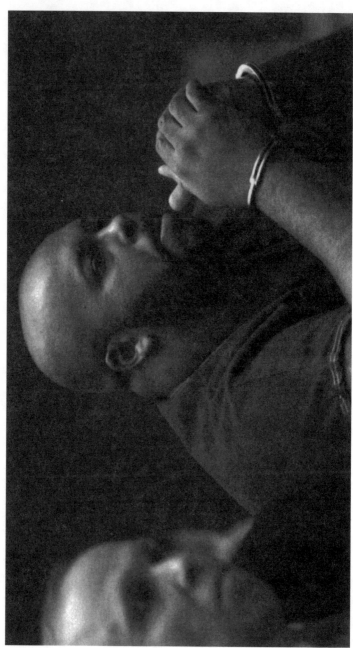

Suge Knight

Chapter Fifteen

Shake It, Baby!

The year Tupac would not live out began with MTV Superstardom. On January 1, 1996, the music video for *California Love* had its world première on MTV – in heavy rotation – serving Tupac to the world on a satellite platter. But *California Love* isn't just a signal of superstardom, it's hiphop's ultimate expression of ambition and indulgence deluxe.

Tupac felt extravagant after Suge Knight visited him in prison with a handwritten contract to join the stable of artists at Death Row Records. 'I know business,' Knight said. 'I know how to take my artists and make them superstar status, and make them get what they deserve.' In collaboration with Dr Dre, Knight had begun an empire based on a new hiphop phase and distinctive sound; it put California hiphop on the map stronger than anything from the Bay area. Tupac was already impressed by it and signed the contract in haste. Knight put up over $1 million in bail, freeing Tupac from institutional bondage and committing him to do three albums for Death Row Records.

'I don't think he had a choice,' Afeni said of the transaction. 'And I'm sure he didn't feel like he had a choice under the circumstances.' No one else was posting bond and Tupac had been ready for freedom a long time – since before birth, Afeni says. Tupac responded to his new boss as if to the big brother he never had – with gratitude and blind trust. Afeni remembers, 'He got out of prison on Thursday and by Thursday night he was in California in the studio. By Friday he had completed seven songs from that double album.'

Afeni's skeptical look-back at Tupac's release comes out of remembering her own release to give birth to her son twenty-four years earlier. Very different circumstances had delivered Tupac from jail to indentured service. And he seemed to respond to his release without suspicion. Though able to turn slick phrases, he didn't find the irony in leaving lockdown and signing to Death Row – a company whose name and commitment suggested no way out.

Fresh from the slammer, he could scoff at the social system that had punished him by embracing the insolence implicit in the name Death Row – a name that spotlighted Black doom, and particularly the Dre-ad fate of the 25 percent of Black youths who languish behind bars.

'When you sign to Death Row you sign for life,' was a cautionary pun among hiphop journalists. Rumors suggested that Tupac had been 'bought' for a million dollars, that his artistic freedom would amount to a sharecropper existence – like Snoop Doggy Dogg's indebtedness that kept him at Death Row even after Dr Dre severed ties with Knight.

Afeni set a high value on freedom. She knew, 'Once someone buys you, they own you.' What she couldn't understand was how Tupac fell for the kind of enticement he had always ragged on.

Go back to 'Young Niggaz' on *Me Against the World* – written and recorded before Tupac's desperation – to find his warning to 'young niggas in a rush to be gangstas.' Tupac's advice: 'Muthafuckaz need to just calm down / And peep what the fuck they want to do with the rest of they life / Before you end your life before you begin your life.' His own words should have cautioned him against his rush to join Death Row. Instead, he saw only the quantum leap up his career would take. Being received by the southern California branch of hiphop meant more than a merger; it promised acceptance in a fraternity. Following all the tension and trouble in New York – the shooting, the rivalry with Biggie, the jail time – Tupac's sense of betrayal was brightened by Knight, who had stepped in like a rescuing knight to offer the rapper a second, bigger chance at stardom.

All Eyez on Me is widely referred to as rap's first double album – a distinction that rightfully belongs to DJ Jazzy Jeff and the Fresh Prince's *I'm the DJ, He's the Rapper*. But Tupac's fourth album was actually rap's first double CD, a major push toward recognition. Sex is the sound of 'California Love,' Tupac's first Number One single. It certifies a level of achievement, of rap triumph and American commercial bliss. It's also the expression/emission of Roger Troutman. And Dr Dre, who produced 'California Love,' gets props for reviving Troutman's 'sound' and fitting it to Tupac's ecstasy. As the lead exponent of the eighties dance group Zapp ('Computer Love' was its big 1986 hit), Troutman innovated a rhythmic vocal distortion that wove through the band's basic funk grooves. His eerily sensual vocal contrasts could be hard to take yet it's one of those signature sounds of individual genius that occur throughout the history of Black pop. (On Scritti Politti's 1989 *Provision*, Green Gartside enlisted Troutman along with Miles Davis to augment his exquisitely high-tech pop deconstructions on the tracks 'Boom! There She Was' and especially 'Sugar and Spice,' where Troutman sang the extremes of nearly inexpressible physical release.)

Troutman's high squeak and low-pitch warbles turn up on

'California Love' to sexualize Dre's particular politics, where prosperity equals orgasm. No one expected a love song from the cold-blooded maestro of gangsta rap but 'California Love' commemorates Tupac's flight west after his East Coast jail bailout. The song celebrates the social haven (goldmine) Dre and Suge Knight invite Tupac to join. It's not the sunny California of teenage fun that The Beach Boys created, but something darker, more evanescent and mercenary. Dre mystifies success as 'love' then raps about California as the locale of his professional and cultural 'triumph.'

There's a mythological – and historical – background to that victory: West Coast hiphop is that area's strongest Black musical achievement. It's an empire of sorts – a dream to the young generation of Black working-class kids whose parents suffered through that Republican community's severe racial redistricting – even after numbers of them had fled to California from worse conditions in the American South. For many, the dream of hiphop success is still deferred. Yet the electricity of a record like 'California Love' shocks the ghost of Tom Joad as it also mocks the real-life efforts of Cesar Chavez and denies the life of George Jackson.

Like Brian Wilson, Dre had tapped into a primal American dream, albeit of a less innocent era. 'F – wit Dre Day' (1993) first claimed this mythological territory when Dre rapped, 'Is it Dre? / That's what they say everyday in LA' and since then he's only blown up bigger. Dre's heinous rap topics (favoring Black self-destruction, class animosity and racial stereotype), his gin-and-juice-soaked vision, still fake Black solidarity by putting forth his own good time to others. Those euphoric beats in 'California Love' aren't an escape from O. J. Simpson's LA but a denial of contemporary stress. And for four minutes, as Dre, Roger and Tupac salute brothers up and down the California map (San Diego, Long Leach, Compton, Watts, San Francisco, Oakland), it's almost convincing. In 'California Love' Dre creates a sense of belonging that neglects rap protest, preferring an affirmation that is vaguely patriotic. He doesn't groove to real-life struggle but to successful capitalist competition – his own genius, granted. Tupac grooved to it big time.

It's a millionaire's selective view, happily ignorant of California's Black history (as partly told in Mike Davis's *City of Quartz*), where only a celebrity like Nat King Cole could break the housing color bar. Roger's role in Dre's victory song shows an ironic, partial alliance – but don't be misled, it's just show business. In 1986, at Zapp's peak, a *Jet* magazine article detailed how Roger and his bandmate-brothers Lester, Larry and Zapp joined with their other siblings Rufus, Janet and Loretta, to build more than 100 low-cost houses in their hometown, Dayton, Ohio. (Accomplished with loans from Warner Bros. and Lefrak Entertainment Company, this is the kind of genuine political action overlooked by the *New York Times*'s recent touting of Suge Knight and his shifting fortunes with Interscope Records.)

Roger told *Jet*: 'The Black community is indeed our responsibility. You're obligated to people if they support you, you're obligated to your roots, no matter what they are. Everyone loves where they come from and if you're not proud of where that is, you should go back and do something about it.'

Dre himself never tries sounding like a politician when party-throwing will do. 'California Love' lowers the bass on the same ear-stunning tintinnabulation that made a hit of 1995's 'Keep Their Heads Ringin'' but turns up the sonic whip. 'Inglewood's always up to no good,' he says ambiguously. And Tupac has accepted the invitation. For both of them, America – California – is a party 'cause it's where they can fulfill their love of money (a false answer to the evils of racism and oppression because it is, of course, the root of such evil). And Tupac hoped to cash in.

'California Love' has a quasi-Republican ethos in the way it substitutes feel-good sentiment for social action. It launched the release of *All Eyez on Me*, with Tupac playing the hyped-up Black ne'er-do-well to perfection. A dull rapper compared to Dre, who masters a functional snarl, Tupac has little to do with this record's beauty – he's still a student to his producer's savvy about the fame business. Dre has the best lines, updating California's sun-fun myth as a defense against depression: 'Like a vest for your jimmy in the city of sex.'

'On a mission for them greens / Lean, mean, money-makin' machine servin' fiends / I been in the game for ten years makin' rap tunes / Ever since honeys was wearin' Sassoons / Now it's 95 and they clock me and watch me / Diamond-shinin', lookin' like I robbed Liberace / It's all good from Diego to the Bay / Your city is the bomb if your city's makin' pay.' Tupac's sex-grunt 'Umpf.' can be heard in the background. Roger's sizzling counterpoints ('Come on, come on' and 'California knows how to party') epitomize how Dre and Tupac get off on the commercialization of Black lawlessness by the sensual distraction of artistic recreation.

Dre gets thrilling effects from mixing fancy JB-horn touts and rumbling piano rhythms with Roger's orgasmic stutters. It's a live and large production, revving up the old notion that gangstas and criminals are sexy into a more precise frenzy. The freedom implicit in their antisocial acts gives them allure. 'California Love' uses Roger's artistic simulation of sexual thrill to proclaim that power Dre must feel every day in LA, knowing he effects the narrow dreams of hiphop's fans and enemies. It's devastating when Roger follows Dre's rap with a one-man chorus that doubly puns:

Shake, Shake it, Baby
Shake, Shake it, Mama
Shake, Shake it, Cali

Hiphop has certainly rocked the authoritarian world of C. Delores Tucker and Bill Bennett; its success can indeed seem earthshaking to musicians benefiting from its quasi-revolution. After The Clash had done its job, frontman Joe Strummer tried to keep going and put out an eighties album titled *Earthquake Weather*, a lame effort still holding on to the idea of creating pop art that can change things aesthetically and for real. It happens that Black American artists who triumph over daily social oppression can automatically achieve the subversive effect white artists construct through theory and illusion. That's how Scritti Politti came to choose Roger – for his inherently subversive art. Dre, obviously, heard only the heritage of pleasure, of endurance, in Roger's vocal blips – seismic evidence of Black life – so he synthesizes it into *material*.

Both Dre and Roger – even Tupac – understand that hiphop's cultural influence has shaken America where it lives and dreams. Movement and money defines the country but the song didn't become a hit until the pop mix – a version that plays to the rhythmic instincts of white listeners as well – was reissued in the summer of 1996. At that point, 'California Love' finally caught on as the stress of the year amped and Dre, Roger and Tupac's release could be felt. 'The track hits your eardrums like slug to your chest,' Dre raps as the music changes the listeners' metabolism, offering instant escape and elevation.

It's elemental, similar to the texture-based smash success of Coolio's 'Gangsta's Paradise' the previous year. These records signify a huge change in pop evolution – not simply in the increase of thematic harshness since Stevie Wonder's 1976 'Pasttime Paradise,' but also in the contemporary pop audience's ignorance of the Wonder tune. The gorgeous string arrangements – unheard for two decades – struck the modem hiphop audience as an unexpected epiphany, giving elegance and elevation to Coolio's litany of ghetto strife. These kids had no idea that Wonder's original song spoke against mid-seventies apathy by critiquing modern political neglect through nostalgia. As the hiphop audience related to the song, they commiserated their own political concern – beyond apathy into a hopeful hopelessness.

This knowledge is central to making sense of the two-hour

playing time of *All Eyez on Me*; it's proof of the energy in Black resignation. *All Eyez on Me* is made to get blunted to; lying back is a requirement for listening to it. Tupac, here, investigates gangsta rap's scary understanding of Black youth's worst instincts – the negativity that hides huge imagination. At first this isn't easy to discern. Dre's use of P-Funk beats is a sign of his own indifference. Emulating James Brown riffs would require more smarts, some confrontation with southern R&B basics rather than George Clinton's protective urban sass. Dre has stated his preference for working with new artists whose voices he can help discover and shape into self-confidence. And although Dre got it up for the stellar 'California Love,' he left Tupac on his own to search for a style.

In Mel Watkins's classic study *The Lyrics of James Brown* (1971), he describes the search that happens within Black pop artistry: 'One's import does not rest with abstract, societally defined positions or postures. Instead it is situation oriented, constantly reassessed, dependent upon the outcome of each personal confrontation and interaction.' In this sense *All Eyez on Me* is a collection of Tupac postures, a one-man filmography of situations, meet-cutes, shoot-outs, money-shots and glamor poses. They may lack Dre's dynamism, but each track is a steady, painstaking display of personal cultural options.

Divided into Books 1 and 2, *All Eyez on Me* parallels Michael Jackson's awesome, intimidating *HIStory*. With *All Eyez on Me* Tupac in the nineties, as much as James Brown in the seventies, affirms his shared acceptance of life's absurdities and jiving. But a close listen to this good-time album reveals a contradiction to Watkins's thesis. In honoring James Brown as a bedrock modern artist, Watkins was speaking of his effect on a more cohesive, saner Black community. Tupac records for a changed, debased America that regales crime and violence as a 'mythic deviation.'

If *All Eyez on Me* is not gangsta rap's best album, it holds position as the form's magnum opus. Every track plays out the gangsta mythology that sustains today's desolate young Black community. Its key subjects are sexual pleasure and male competition, but where James Brown once embodied these themes (Watkins credits Brown's performance as 'authentic' and his lyrics with 'meaning that transcends mere sexuality [with] social meaning [that is] readily understood by Black audiences'), Tupac merely mimes them. Only a few of these tracks are so deeply imagined that one can say Tupac embodies their subject. His contradictory compassion and disdain from song to song makes the album a chain of oddly cut links.

Book 1

Ambitionz As a Ridah – 'I'm on a meal ticket mission,' Tupac begins, observing ghetto chaos: 'Niggas is jealous / Deep inside they wanna be me.' 'It was my ambition to rise above these jealous motherfuckers.' To dramatize the disorder, producer Dat Nigga Daz keeps Tupac's voice level with the bass mix. Chaos and competition.

All Bout U – 'Every other city we go, every other video no matter where we go, I see the same ho's' says the chorus, made up of Tupac, Snoop Doggy Dogg and Nate Dogg. It's the flip of DJ Quik. 'I'm a thug nigga, I love niggas,' plies the fantasy of hiphop rollin'. It's more ambitioning but never sanctimonious: Snoop mentions seeing the same 'bitch' in Warren G and Tupac videos, also seen at the Million Man March. Lyrically, the put-down crosses gender, as in Apache's 'Gangsta Bitch.' Its ambivalence puts 'You're So Vain' in the context of ghetto jealousy.

Skandalouz – Turned on by skeezers, Tupac puts them down. Shame rears its head. Look out: he's scandalized.

Got My Mind Made Up – 'Get off my coat / Clearin' my throat' – a blues reference via The Beastie Boys. The past is alive: 'Smilin' faces deceive,' Redman says in a conversation with Tupac, Dat Nigga Daz, Kurupt and Method Man. An echoing drum beat measures their reinforced distrust. Each bro builds up the other's paranoia.

How Do U Want It – 'Comin' up as a nigga in a cash game / Living in the fast lane' – a sequel to Jodeci's *The Concert, The Afterparty, The Hotel*, a landmark of the pimpology that infects hiphop. Jodeci's K-Ci sings the sexual metaphor of what is really a fuck-off to Tupac's critics. The rhyme 'Delores Tucker you a motherfucker instead of tryin' to help a nigga you destroy a brother' begins a list of sucker politicians. It makes subversive use of Quincy Jones's 'Body Heat.' Producer Johnny J finds it a classical expression of Black achievement.

2 of Amerikaz Most Wanted – 'Nothing but a gangsta party,' Snoop agrees with Tupac. Happy to stroll along Death Row, they dive into the stereotypes that previously chafed them.

No More Pain – 'When I die I want to be a living legend.' Alize and Cristal set the mood for a martyr's consumption and belligerence: 'They shot me five times but real niggas don't die / Death is reincarnation / I came to bring the pain hardcore to the brain.' Funereal elegance borrowed from Jodeci producer DeVante Swing. There's a correlation between the slick life of amoral sensuality and immoral revenge, 'Retaliation is a must.' Death is the only relief Tupac offers, cheering 'Thug Life!' at the end.

Heartz of Men – Tupac tells Suge Knight to watch him get even. 'I'm gonna start diggin' to these nigga's chest. Friends vs. Enemies.' And 'It's a dirty game / Y'all gotta be careful who you fuck with.' He doubles the meaing of 'fuck with' but the complication is spoken more to himself. Reference to Mr Makaveli introduces his vengeful *alterego*. Richard Pryor's 'That Nigger's Crazy' sample makes comic drama out of fearful retaliation.

Life Goes On – In a mellower mood, a reminiscence song.

'How many brothers fell victim to the street / Rest in peace young nigga there's a heaven for a G.' Well set up, with a grungy detail, 'I got your name tatted on my arm, so we both bond till the day I die.' A key song, if only for the way sentiment interrupts the troublesome parlaying of responsibility to 'the street.' Still, the musical sway can carry a listener to maudlin softness. It recalls the way Ice Cube's 'Dead Homiez' pioneered this sense of loss.

Only God Can Judge Me – 'In my mind, I'm a blind man doin' time' 'They say it's the white man I should fear, but it's my own kind doin' all the killin' here.' Zigzag beat cushion for Tupac's simple delivery, the points touch neatly. 'And all my memories is seein' brothers bleed' or 'I'm havin' nightmares, homicidal fantasies.' Movin' from Geto Boys to Prince ('Cuz even doves cry but does God care?') Tupac gathers together pop's most accomplished tropes of wonderment. It's an effort to make sense but there is no intellectual movement here; no investigation. Shallowness comes in blurts.

Tradin' War Stories – 'A military mind / A criminal grind.' Makaveli comes up again: 'Mama sent me to play with the drug dealers' – if this is true, it's a shock, full of leisurely presented resentment. Dramacyde's soft, feminine background attempts soothing like the strings of 'Gangsta's Paradise.' There's a good sense of drama in Mike Mosley's and Rick Rock's production. The self-sentimentalized invoking of 'street soldiers' adds to camaraderie, but it still distorts the truth of daily miserableness. It's the kind of put-on that only works when done in passing conversation, but as an extended metaphor ('Outlaws on the rise / Jealous niggas I despise / Look in my eyes') this song pinpoints animosity, not the sense of aggrieved sides. 'It's what players do,' he lets us know. For him, playin' is all.

California Love (RMX) – Slowed down from the magnificent pop mix, it fits a Buddha buzz. No version of this record is bad; the plus here is Roger's coda. 'Shake it¡ Cali,' his computer whines – to his ideal woman? L. L. Cool J's? Or maybe even to the earth that moved under Carole King's feet?

I Ain't Mad at Cha – 'Whatever it takes to get you niggas out the hood.' That's superficial encouragement, but there's tangible love here, from the words of forgiveness to the blessed Stevie Wonder-style humming in back. Better than 'Tradin' War Stories,' it details boyish squabbling in proper proportion. This is at least a genuine youth's insight, including his pleas to Mama.

What'z Ya Phone # – Riding the groove of The Time's '777-9311,' Tupac's comical lewdness pivots on his sly use of 'fuck with me' to make phone sex sizzle – a distanced bluff of prowess. It's an inadvertent metaphor for a recording artist's put-on. 'I'm fixin' to come over there,' he says, but as most Tupac fans must attest, he never comes.

Book 2

Can't C Me – In retrospect this song would seem to fuel 'Tupac is Alive!' speculation, but it's really a boast of slipperiness, shamelessly suggesting some craven deliberateness in Tupac's changeable persona and point of view. No chameleon pleasure in versatile self-image is evident, but Dre makes this track funk harder than anything else on the album. At least a tough joke, if not a good one.

Shorty Wanna Be a Thug – 'Said he wanna be / One day he gonna be,' goes this bedtime story. But in narrating a thug life saga, Tupac reveals more about his own ambition than any appeal he might have for youngbloods. Still, Dre's *The Chronic* told this story better in 'L'il Ghetto Boy.'

Holla at Me – In the person of his left-behind homeys, Tupac fears for his own estrangement. 'Gotta be careful can't let the evil of the money trap me' is a class-war principle, not often stated. Although about self, it can be heard – especially in the jail verse – as Tupac's most empathetic composition.

Wonda Why They Call U Bitch – 'You leave your kids with your mama cuz you headin' for the club,' Tupac admonishes bad young mothers. And 'See, I loved you like a sister but you died too quick' has no compassion. This is moralism, not understanding. Even when he notes, 'Dear Miss C. Delores Tucker, you keep stressin' me / I thought you wanted to know why we call them bitches.' But without realizing any common concern with Miss Tucker, this flipside of 'Keep Ya Head Up' shows he can be just as severe and insensitive as his own critics.

When We Ride – 'My name is Makaveli,' Tupac jokes before flaunting the names Castro, Khadafi, Mussolini as trouble-making inspirations. Insipid, but at least DJ Pooh makes the track pump.

Thug Passion – A reworking of Roger's 'Computer Love,' so there's some R&B flow. Despite the yen of the female voices – Dramacydal, Jewell and Storm – it's stuck at playing out a boy's fantasy.

Picture Me Rollin' – 'Why niggas look mad? Y'all supposed to be happy.' Sometimes Tupac's opening lines contain his only complexity. Here he barely sustains the irony in this more serious retake of 'Ambitionz as a Ridah.' His harried voice sounds skint opposite Danny Boy's secure baritone, but the whole thing's about image vs. reality, as in the fade-out taunts to the district attorney and police.

Check Out Time – Maybe art imitates life but because the sleaze of on-the-road sex occupies this percolating track, it keeps the husky sounds of guest rappers Kurupt and Syke focused. Minor, superficial but smooth.

Ratha Be Ya Nigga – 'I don't want to be yo' man, I want to be ya nigga,' he says, trumping The Beatles. 'So I can get drunk and smoke weed all day.' Tupac attempts to eroticize Black stereotypes that he half believes. His boast, 'A boss player, freaky, motherfucker ghetto dick,' doesn't rise above racism but goes limp before its restrictions.

All Eyez on Me – Self-consciousness: 'The fans is watchin' / Niggas plottin' to get me.' 'I told the judge I was raised wrong / And that's why I play shit.' Not so much a coming clean as self-protective bluster. It's the knowingness of role-playing that makes the beat's monotony wear in – like a threat.

Run tha Streeetz – Long missing in action Michel'le sings support ('I'll be waiting for you until you get through'). But the strength of her voice contradicts. Stuck in the background, she sneaks in passionate impatience, giving the lie to so much accumulated fronting.

Ain't Hard to Find – 'Waldo?, Waldo?' says one of the crowd, E-40, B-Legit, C-Bo and Richie Rich. A casual track that affirms we-are-everywhere in Tupac's offhand rhythm. A no-brainer.

Heaven Ain't Hard 2 Find – Feet, balls and mind on the ground, Tupac rejects pie-in-the-sky for the groove he can get right here and now. The simple, loping beat allows him to deliver his best rap. It's his least sentimental track. Not a song for soldiers but a reach for contentment.

All Eyez on Me's centerpiece CD artwork is a ghetto primitive painting of Tupac and four mates confronting a short-skirted hottie – a reference to the sexual assault that got him into trouble, it creates its own mythology. How can one read this representation of a liquored-up, flirtatious, gang-fronting Tupac, except as the opposite of an idealization – a mean enshrinement of rude living? That puts the graphic in line with the rest of the album. It's a well-programmed, long-winded small statement. 'You think we all dogs,' he accuses on the album's closing track, but it's part of a complication that Tupac was too enamored of to examine. There's not much more ambition here than simply to impress by size – the album was written and recorded too quickly to have been thought out beyond simple tracks and talented invited guests.

Tupac's intention with *All Eyez on Me* was to rise brazenly from the lower depths of prison with an apotheosis – a deluxe street album. But that's a contradiction in terms, showing either the artist's grandiose silliness or his incapacity. The fact that he could command Death Row's resources to produce a two-disc act of hubris says more about the ambition than it signifies art – or the understanding of life and humanity that art reveals. Grandstanding, *All Eyez on Me* is impressive, but it speaks less powerfully than simple honesty.

Reborn on two levels, Tupac's rapping in *All Eyez on Me* took on the polyphonic flow that was distinctive to Dre productions; plus, his approach to 'what they say everyday in LA' got even wilder. The Death Row principle of artist behavior, based on movie star/crime star emulation, gave Tupac more opportunity to make theater out of the 'revolutionary' urge that seemed no longer possible in the political world. Youthful Black activism – essentially a dream of the past – was never more to Tupac than a role to play. He jumped at this moment like an understudy leaping to the lucky break of a stand-in matinée performance. Death Row, an offshoot of Interscope Records (the label founded by producer Jimmy Iovine, an engineer renowned for his pristine work with such seventies rock icons as Bruce Springsteen and Tom Petty), took the idea of corporate independence a step further, prompting a renegade attitude and image that suited Tupac's need for audacity.

Tupac's grim impudence wryly contrasted the dreams of success Dre and Knight sought. It also gave tickling, troubling nuance to the LA attitude of prosperity and glory that came with the changes Dre instituted to make hiphop an unabashed celebration of power and greed. What's often missed in considerations of Death Row rap is the amount of conscious nihilism being used as an emotional element, if not an operational principle. You could call it jailbird sensibility for its acceptance of demeaning circumstances, fighting degradation with deprecation. That's subtly encoded in the West Coast etymology of 'nigger' into 'nigga.' Death Row rap internalizes Black youth's affront at their social mistreatment with gallows humor. Part of its purposefulness is in ratifying the perhaps necessary psychological trick of finding a way to cope with disparagement, and humor does it fine. The wit of owning 'Death Row' — as both a term and label — comes from the reclaimed power of renaming oneself, appropriating government's right to judge and designate. This may be a screwed-up response to authoritarian pressure, but conscious nihilism isn't as pathetic as the unconscious, unrecognized, untraceable sort. Dre clearly understands the socio-economic conditions he must oppose and his single-minded success ethic demonstrates a cynicism that shouldn't be confused with nihilism. Death Row Records takes a capitalist approach to nihilism, finding it marketable and relishing the piddling amount of defiance it permits. It fills up that moral hollow where Black pop's heart used to be (you could hear it in such empowering songs of endearment as The Funky Four Plus One's 'That's the Joint,' De La Soul's 'Me, Myself and I' and Son of Bazerk's 'One Time for the Rebel').

Death Row's hardened yet affectionate treatment of Black experience matches the complexity of *All Eyez on Me,* where Tupac responds to his own condition, searching for love though deprived of peace. Singing about his own death in 'No More Pain' seemed to be the only way he could give clues to feeling enslaved. 'Gotta be careful can't let the evil of the money trap me,' he said on 'Holler at Me.' His convoluted affection and aggression cannot be ignored. They remain part of African American cultural habits, summoning grace during the effrontery of jesting.

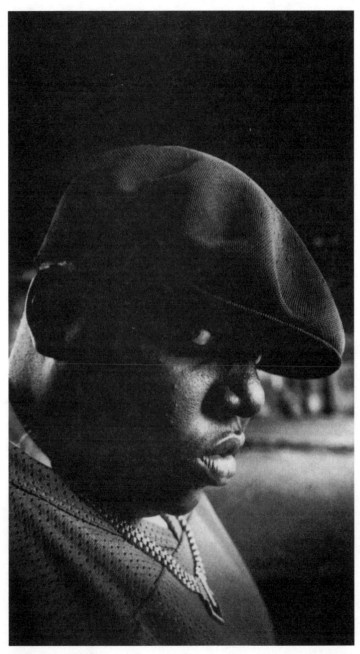

Notorious B.I.G.

Chapter Sixteen

Makaveli

Tupac learned the Westside sign: closing his thumb in his palm, crossing his middle fingers like a temptress's legs and letting his index finger and pinkie point out to form a proud 'W.' That salute decorates the cover of *All Eyez on Me*, but pledging California as his home wasn't so simple. Tupac found the southern California style different from both New York and the Bay area. 'I feel like a new kid,' an engineer heard him say when he stepped into the studio to record 'California Love.'

Tupac should have taken heed. Back in the Digital Underground days, Money B warned him, 'No new niggas. You feel me? 'Cause new niggas always bring problems. You don't know them, you don't know their background. You don't know what they're about . . .'

But Tupac was up to his headscarf in new: a new label, a new *alter ego*, a new surliness. Through Makaveli, Tupac responded to Death Row's new ruthlessness with a fever. Suge Knight's excitable routines – hard-ass business negotiations, reckless high-rolling – were a source of dismay even to hyperactive Tupac. Tupac's old friends were mystified to see him taking up with this 'new nigga,' without distancing himself from the combination of Gangsterism and Industry. Incensed by his scraps with Biggie Smalls, resentful from Dr Dre's Death Row defection, Tupac's loyalty to Suge Knight only grew. This new nigga, Makaveli, presented a harsher, even more conflicted Tupac than the Bay area crew ever knew.

Scott Gordon, an old school Oakland-based radio DJ who had known him from the moment he joined the Digital Underground tour, tried to sort out the enigma of Tupac's new surliness: 'Suge Knight, he a businessman to all degrees from the street to the major level. To me, 'Pac made a deal with the Devil. 'Pac had everything. He got shot in New York and lived. He talked shit about some of the biggest motherfuckers in New York and he lived. He went to jail, got out on money that Suge Knight gave up. Cars, gold, girls, women, he worked with the biggest artists in the country, movies. He had everything in his hands. And to me, that's something that the Devil gives you. God don't give you all of that. Especially if you sit there and worship money. Money is not what God gives you, it's what the Devil gives you.'

Reverend Daughtry felt Tupac's turmoil rose from a spiritual crisis: 'What appeared to us to be his confused, troubled, complex behavior, maybe, maybe it all stemmed from his fleeing from God. His fighting, his struggling, was at bottom not so much against society. He was running away from God. Like Jonah of the Bible, he ran away from God. He created trouble and problems on the ship upon which he tried to escape. The people on the ship decided to throw him to the sea, where a big fish was there to swallow him up, and once he confessed, agreed to do God's will, the fish spit him up on shore and Jonah did what God wanted. Tupac ran away. He was thrown overboard but there was no big fish to swallow him up and spit him on shore. Or maybe another way of saying it is, when he was swallowed up by the jail system and spit back out on the streets, unlike Jonah, he ... well ...'

Both of these classic explanations may be behind Tupac telling people, after *All Eyez on Me*, 'I'm a living legend.' Recognizing his hiphop achievements, he willed status to himself and created a stage name to illustrate it: Makaveli – an ultra-slick reference to the late-fifteenth and early-sixteenth century Florentine philosopher Niccolò Machiavelli, best known for political writings which declared power amoral and justified any means to get it. Now Tupac reveled in the double consciousness Reverend Daughtry referred to in religious terms and W. E. B. DuBois wrote about, in secular terms, in his 1903 work *The Souls of Black Folk*:

> The Negro is a sort of seventh son, born with a veil, and gifted with second-sight in this American world – a world which yields him no true self-consciousness, but only lets him see himself through the revelation of the other world. It is a peculiar sensation, this double-consciousness, this sense of always looking at one's self through the eyes of others, of measuring one's soul by the tape of a world that looks on in amused contempt and pity. One ever feels his twoness – an American, a Negro; two souls, two thoughts, two unreconciled strivings; two warring ideals in one dark body, whose dogged strength alone keeps it from being torn asunder.

Generations of Black Americans – the Panthers and hiphop artists included – have responded in different ways to DuBois's insight, some attempting to prove it wrong or obsolete; but almost all find his wisdom hard to refute. Even a character as radically conceived as Makaveli fits the description. The artist formerly known as Tupac *acts* instinctively on the confusions of double-consciousness and the anxieties of modern wickedness, whereas Tupac originally only *reacted* to them

Bay area rapper MC Manus, who had moved to Los Angeles since Tupac was in Digital Underground, spoke to Tupac during the recording of *The Don Killuminati the Seven-Day Theory*. They had a heart-to-heart: 'I could feel his pain. He was committed to life even though he used to say he was "commuted." He was set on slanging the bullshit that goes down, but people was tryin' to get him away from the real. I seen this happen to rappers before and told him. He said, "I know Mack, you the king of thieves," and I said "Blood, let me tell you your future with Death Row in a minute or less. I'll tell you what comes next. They moguls, man, and the moguls want a human sacrifice. They see a young rapper out here wantin' to make money and they say, "Look at that nigga. He's young, he's hungry – he's perplexed." That's what they say. And they take away the best years of your life. You might think it's all in good fun. But it's up to you to keep your shit clean – get your shit together – if you want to laugh at *them* in the end. If I were you I'd change my name again. They don't care what they do to you, believe me.'

As MC Manus saw Tupac's situation, he had come to feel like a double man In MC Manus's words, 'He don't need no mirror to talk to hisself. He was conversatin' in his own head.' MC Manus was shocked when Tupac said of Makaveli and the whole hiphop image, 'It's up to me to decide when my public image becomes the real thing – whatever the real thing is.'

A popular quote among Tupac graveworshippers is, 'I never had a record *before* I made a record.' In a nation where you're unlikely to be arrested if you're rich that means exactly nothing. As Makaveli, he intends to justify his unfair bad rep. It's a defensive position – Tupac considered Makaveli a political move, akin to Black impatience and aggravation – and he explained this analogy on MTV: 'If you know in this hotel room they have food every day and I knock on the door. *Every day* they open the door to let me see the party, let me see that they throwin' salami, throwin' food around but telling me there's no food. *Every day*. I'm standing outside trying to sing my way in – "We are weak, please let us in. We are weak, please let us in." After about a week that song is gonna change to, "We hungry, we need some food." After two, three weeks it's like, "Give me some of the food! I'm breakin' down the door." After a year it's like, "I'm pickin' the lock, comin' through the door blastin'." It's like, "I'm hungry!" You reached your level, you don't want any more. We asked ten years ago, we were askin' with the Panthers, we were askin' in the Civil Rights Movement. Now those people who were askin' are all dead or in jail, so what are we gonna do?

'And we shouldn't be angry! And the raps that I'm rapping to my community shouldn't be filled with rage? They shouldn't be filled with the same atrocities that they gave to me? The media they don't talk about it, so in my raps I have to talk about it, and it just seems foreign because there's no one else talking about it.' It's strange rhetoric for a successful man, but Tupac pumped himself up on it.

The disingenuousness in this interview makes it the most fascinating and revealing Tupac ever gave. Raised to see deprivation as the only Black reality, Tupac's complaint about success confessed the class envy most rappers hide.

'It's like bein' the last person alive. After three days you can't do anything. What can I do, where can I go? There's no Black neighborhood where Black people who have the same amount of money as me. There's richer and there's poorer. There's no just, you know, "I did a movie, got a little bit of money, livin' OK' Black neighborhood, so I gotta live in a white neighborhood. I don't fit it, so that's hell. It's hell when you can't be around your peers. All my life I grew up around Black people, poor people. But I can't live around poor people now cuz they'll rob me. And why would they rob me? Because they're starvin', cuz there's no money here. But they telling me now that I've made a little money, I have to move here."'

'Here' was Sherman Oaks, where Tupac had bought a home for his mother. Located on the other side of Beverly Hills, it was the upscale suburb many in the Death Row stable moved to – out of Long Beach, out of the ghetto, to a place that marked some degree of affluence and attainment. But not a place where Tupac felt at home. For an ex-Panther and her children, Sherman Oaks represented dislocation and entrapment in a way that few understood.

'No one's ever trying to deal with this section,' he said. 'They're just movin' away from it and we're gonna have more stars comin' from the ghetto and they're gonna all move this way.' This has no connection to the political ideas Tupac was weaned on. As Makaveli he attempts to resolve his conflict between politics and showbiz based solely on impulse. Tupac always said, 'People who think I'm like two different people – a wild gangsta and a caring, sensitive young black man – don't really know me.' They failed to recognize that everyone shows aspects of themselves at different times, to different people. Acting on Machiavelli's popular credo 'The end justifies the means' (from his book *The Prince*), Tupac concocted Makaveli to mess with the heads of people too thoughtless to bother wondering who he really was.

The clues are throughout *All Eyez on Me*: his ambition to rise above 'jealous motherfuckers,' his hot sense of friends vs. enemies and, most of all, his speculation on a posthumous identity where 'Only God Can Judge Me.' On the song 'When We Ride,' Tupac equates Makaveli with American political foes, but fans didn't pick up on the message. Given Tupac's many conflicts, it only resulted in confusion and mystery.

The Makaveli album, *The Don Killuminati the Seven-Day Theory*, doesn't give an exact answer. It's an incomplete statement; at first it seems a mistake in progress, starting off with the kind of fabricated news broadcast Public Enemy made an art form (and that Tupac imitated on *Me Against the World*). This one is a bulletin of label wars, a statement of the confusion Tupac, like Jonah, is trying to swim through.

'Hey-Yea!' Tupac sings at one point during 'I Bomb First (My Second Reply).' It's the only joyous sound he ever put on record, yet he seems bugged, perhaps high (on mayhem). Since joining Death Row something awful took hold of his aesthetic: a new joy in fighting people as powerless as himself.

Hiphop's good times are far behind Tupac now (Harry Allen had situated his growth as 'on the cusp of Public Enemy's decline and N.W.A.'s rise') and he sank into vitriol. His new vision ('Some say the game is all corrupted / Fuck this shit') is stated as a prayer on 'Hail Mary.'

As Makaveli, Tupac assumes his nastiest characterization yet. It's a persona game, like the imp Gemini that Prince introduced on 'Partyman.' But there's no balance between Tupac's street vision and moral vision. It's unsettling because, as Leopold Senghor described Negro culture, 'Art is not a separate activity, in itself or for itself: it is a social activity, a technique of living, a handicraft in fact.' Tupac always believed in hiphop's function as a poetic description of the ways Black people live.

Paula Giddings got close to Tupac's rationale when she examined the work of sixties street poet Don L. Lee:

> It is through this 'technique of living' that Lee hopes to redefine herohood in the Black community. For he remembers his childhood heroes in the Black Bottom section of Detroit, where he grew up. They were the pimps and the pushers – Black people who exercise some control over their environment and their lives. But in the final analysis their effect was negative to the community. So Lee frequently writes about those who have benefited the community while he himself exercises an almost Gandhian self-discipline.

Makaveli's interest in stepped-up violence, portraying hostility as the nature of Black existence, illustrates the futility Tupac felt. 'Toss It Up,' one of the album's better tracks rips off Blackstreet's 'No Diggity.' It's always good to hear that piano vamp again – even distilled into itchy synthesized noises. The technique is used nihilistically: 'No Longer Dre Day – Arrividerci' 'We untouchable!' he screams, alluding to Death Row's new label description now used to replace 'Out da Gutta,' but also claiming invincibility. There ought to be some sense made of all this in 'To Live and Die in LA.' It is an assessment, of sorts, a tribute to the good and bad ways of living in the city of angels. Yet, throughout the album Tupac keeps falling back into ghetto meanness, brazenly mocking the kind of call-in radio shows his fans follow. A female radio DJ asks callers, 'This is Street Signs. How do you feel when you hear a record like Tupac's new one? Don't you feel like that creates tension between East and West? He's talking about killing people . . . I had sex with your wife – not in those words . . . he's talking about, "I want to see you deceased!"'

That's more like what Naughty by Nature's Treach actually said after Tupac's death on *Street Soldiers*, Lisa Evers's rap show on New York's HOT-97. 'People who think Tupac deserved to die should die!' Treach was defending Tupac's memory but he, too, lacks cunning; as Brother O.P.P. he continues the animosity that brought Tupac grief in the first place.

Makaveli is a mythic figure conjured to justify the same illogic; he promises, 'We may fight amongst each other but I tell you this: We burn this bitch down [if you] get us pissed.' It's a gang-war anthem for street soldiers without a strategy.

Prior to the release of *The Resurrection*, the Houston rappers Geto Boys had their own internal friction (less publicized than Tupac's feuds with Biggie Smalls and Sean Puffy Combs). In one of the greatest moments on *The Resurrection*, the ridiculous nature of hiphop squabbles is put into perspective:

> *It's GB and Willie D reunited*
> *Sendin' niggas back to the studio*
> *To get they shit tighter*
> *The folks said it wouldn't happen again*
> *But we sat down and settled our differences like men*

And if that sounds too namby-pamby, Willie D talks even plainer:

> *We put the bullshit behind us*
> *Cause fuckin' up money ain't a plus*
> *It's a minus*

Tupac could have learned from Geto Boys, 'the ultimate good of brotherhood.' But Makaveli has little time for brotherhood. He capitalizes on the unfunny viciousness of the vaunted game 'the dozens' – though it's good to hear Tupac put Nas in his place:

> *Think he live like me*
> *Talk about he left the hospital*
> *Takin' five like me*
> *You livin' fantasies nigga*
> *I reject yo deposit*
> *We shoot Dre's punk ass*
> *Now we out of the closet.*

Those clever words most impress listeners who probably have no sense of how urban Black revolutionary poetry once made its effect civilly, before it was a million-dollar safe bet. It's worth knowing what Don L. Lee (who changed his name to Haki Madhubuti) knew about Black art, as Paula Giddings put it in her 1971 study of Lee (*From a Black Perspective*): 'That which does not edify Black survival tends to nullify it.'

One result is what Tupac considers 'Blasphemy.' The track with that title isn't really anti-religious, but anti-reality. 'Have you ever seen a crackhead? That's eternal fire.' 'Mama, tell me, am I wrong? Is God just another cop waiting to beat my ass if I don't go pop?' 'They say Jesus is a kind man but he should understand . . . I hope God can see my heart is pure.' All these suggestions go against good-sense notions of living such as the Geto Boys achieve on their album which better suggests the chastened despair of genuine conversion Tupac was after but never managed to find.

Humility ought to be behind all this trash talk, but in what seems like an improvised process of recording this album, Tupac doesn't risk tenderness until he wears down his vapidity. The shift occurs with a clever duel between bass guitar and mandolin on 'Life of an Outlaw' – a duel between gruffness and sweetness. The musicians know more than the rapper about the values at stake in hiphop's moral dilemmas. 'It's hard to be a man running with my guns in hand' go the lyrics. But while the 'guns in hand' part falsifies the contemplation, the musical instruments are the great persuader.

Next, on 'Just Like Daddy,' Makaveli assumes a patriarchal role. Tupac and his crew rap bedroom endearments as though the only time they feel responsible to sisters is when sexing them. He's circled a long time around this raw realization of what constitutes manhood. And though it's a naïvely primal notion, at least it's a sign of Tupac paying attention to what's outside his own body.

It's in the daddy role, however, that Makaveli seems most traditional, still presuming male authority – as if Afeni had struggled for nothing. 'Just Like Daddy' is the wishful promise of a boy longing for Daddy rather than a man pledging his commitment. (Another cut, 'Me and My Girlfriend,' is no different; it just sets the sentiments of Apache's infamous 'Gangster Bitch' to a Flamingo guitar.) To have wound up at this stage of parental envy says a lot about Tupac's personal confusion, but it also limits the love raps in 'Just Like Daddy' – fervent, descriptive and plentiful though they are – to what it might help to call sexual illiteracy – more gender division and regressed priorities.

Having gotten this low, on 'Krazy' Tupac blisses out and visions start to materialize:

Puffin' on lye and dreams
I see Bloods and Crips lookin' for a better way
My brothers and sisters it's time to build cuz even thug niggas pray
Hopin' God hear me
I entered the game
Look how much I changed
I'm no longer innocent
Casualties of fame
Made a lot of money

Seen a lot of places
And I swear I seen a peaceful smile on my mama's face
When I gave her the keys to her own house
'This yo land
Yo only son done became a man'
Watchin' time fly
I love my people do or die
June One-Six-Seven was the day
Mama pushed me out her womb said
Nigga get paid.

That's about as good as Don L. Lee ever was. These lines ring autobiographic the same way as 'Dear Mama' but with a more completely realized pathos. This is the post-jail album *All Eyez on Me* was too rushed to be.

How can a son of revolution, who means well, be so misguided? It's a bigger question than Tupac himself could answer. But the truth may lie in the confusions of race and class that Tupac would not – and the people who loved him will not – see through. The same rough themes are burdened by his limited stock of emotions. It's the new sense of profit, admitting he got a little something out of the system besides grief, that makes the apologetic 'Krazy' such a humane recitation.

Rash young listeners may thrive on Tupac's invective; older and thoughtful listeners may share his disgust but back off from the songs themselves because they illustrate such a cramped way of thinking. A critical response to Tupac has to push past the easy instinct to regret the artist's waste of talent. Fans who are comfortable pining for Tupac do a disservice to themselves, hobbling their own capacity to cope with the world, settling in to the confusion that only got Tupac nowhere – unable to reconcile with the mixed-up human legacy that was left to him. Pop doesn't have to be this thick-witted to be passionate. Much of it offers fine scrutiny of life's complications while bursting with life.

When asked what he was best known for, Tupac gave an encompassing answer: 'My big mouth. My big mouth. I got a big mouth. I can't help it, I talk from my heart, I'm real. You know what I'm sayin'? Whatever comes, comes. But it's not my fault. I'm trying to find my way in the world. I'm trying to be somebody instead making money off everybody, you know what I'm sayin'? So I go down paths that haven't been traveled before. And I usually mess up, but I learn. I come back stronger. I'm not talkin' ignorant. So obviously I put thought into what I do. So I think my mouth and my controversy. I haven't been out of the paper since I joined Digital Underground. And that's good for me cuz I don't want to be forgotten. If I'm forgotten then that means I'm comfortable and that means I think everything is OK.'

We can't forget the complicated, grateful/sorry part that money plays in Tupac's warped vision. Even though he forgets what James Brown knew – 'Money won't change you / But time will take you on.' During the eighties Republican revolution a white pop band, The Brains, misread the signs and made 'Money Changes Everything,' a critically acclaimed record that defied Brown with the wish of the acquisitive. Black culture with its feet on the ground used to know better. Tupac, in his angry delirium, behaved as if decades of Black perserverence and wisdom had taught him nothing of that wisdom. He thought change could be brought about by swaggering, pseudo-political exhortations, but he left Black depression where it was before.

Tupac also said he was best known for: '. . . taking five bullets. Surviving, I'm known as a survivor now, I hope so. For the jail thing, bullets and everything, controversies and everything. I hope so, and I want, in the future, I want people to be talking about me like, you know, "Remember when he was real bad? Remember when Tupac was real bad?" Everybody changes, everybody becomes better people. We all should get that chance. I just want my chance.'

Makaveli's final track, 'Against All Odds', leads back to

nowhere – Black antagonism. And you know how that ends. The line 'Last words to a bitch nigga, why you lie?' are some of the last words Tupac ever recorded. When he rasps them out, his voice is tight. It doesn't bear pain the way a gospel veteran like Pop Staples or a Southern rapper like Brad (Scarface) Jordan does. Makaveli's voice is clenched with urban tension, which makes that line reverberate back at him and his listeners.

Will Tupac's death make a difference in the way rappers and fans confuse money love with the race bravado? Can grief lift them out of their dog-eat-dog narcosis? The rivalry between Tupac and Puffy, Dre, Biggie, Nas and Mobb Deep is unimportant next to the tension that encloses them all. Crabs in a barrel. One more rapper misunderstood. One more Black man in a box.

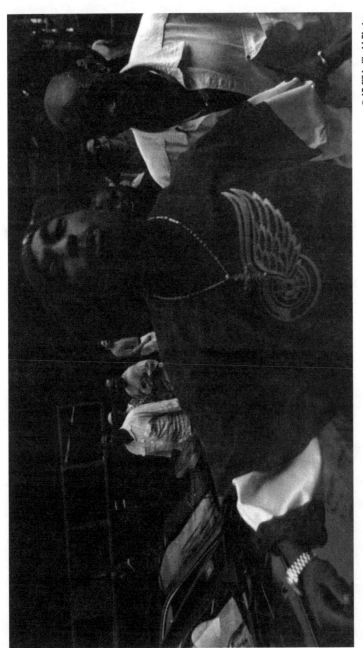

Chapter Seventeen

Your Entertainment, My Reality

Will Tupac be remembered as a stereotype or as his own man? Money B, who knew Tupac, understood these pressures. 'The media, they all say, "Gangster rapper Tupac, blah, blah, blah." But if you knew Tupac, he was real sensitive, real intelligent, real political. You know, if you had a deep conversation with him, he'd get off into some deep shit wit'chu. But at the same time, don't try to play him. You know what I'm saying? He could go there . . . So the thing with 'Pac and the media is, the media never wants to know you. They wanna find something to jump on and run it. You know how it is.'

But most hiphop fans don't know. Eager to find their culture – their lives – validated in the media, they have accepted its distortion both in reporting and in the industry-controlled making of hiphop.

When Tupac told *The City Sun*, 'We need to report our own truth,' he spoke for the growing awareness among rappers that media untruths must be challenged. That's why Poppa LQ, a young rapper from Houston, chose *Your Entertainment, My Reality* as the title of his 1996 debut album: to announce the strain felt by Black American males in this period of intense media scrutiny and dwindling political sympathy. The slogan applies as much to the rapper's exploited role in the music industry as to the growing confusion in the media between sociopolitical news and entertainment, all too often starring Black folks in an ongoing saga of pathos and transgression. Civilians become performers. Performers become celebrities. Celebrities become criminals. Word becomes bondage. In what they say for their own defense, or what journalists say to manipulate the public's perception, an individual can be glorified or demonized, exonerated or judged guilty.

Tupac's reality became public entertainment in the era's ultimate stageshow – the courts. And he played to it in a number of court cases that reality-checked his wild-entertainer antics. Unfortunately Tupac's infractions are rarely seriously considered by the mainstream as the result of plain old bad judgment or sheer bad luck. Only a hiphop publication like Long Island's *The Agenda* would dare to reason, 'The only "ignorant thing" Tupac may have done is used fk'd up judgment and make some ill-self-advised decisions. He, unlike a lot of other "brothas," has been open about his deep love for niggas.'

A repetition of the demonizing pattern has become a hiphop rite of passage – the mug shot replacing the cheesecake photo of young Hollywood hopefuls. This is how the mainstream media constructs demeaning views of hiphop stars. 'That's bullshit, they gotta erase that gun out of my hand!' Tupac had said in 1990 when Paramount Pictures turned the airbrush on advertisements for *Juice*. The incident stayed with him as an example of how media constructs and 'corrects' its images. Even critiques of Tupac's own art have been used as part of the distortion.

'Easy Target' is *Rolling Stone*'s obituary piece. Written by Mikal Gilmore, it represents the rock-crit establishment's old-guard fear and loathing of hiphop. Implicit in the essay is the assumption that Black street talk exemplifies some intense, primal hatred and hostility. Gilmore takes 'Hit 'Em Up' literally as Tupac's threat on the lives of anyone who's down with the East Coast – as if that might even include the staff of *Rolling Stone*. There's no room in Gilmore's reading of 'Hit 'Em Up' for the possibility that a Black artist has enough cunning to pretend anger in a performance. In addition to dragging out tired old Staggerlee stereotypes to parlay Tupac's death into rock-n-roll copy, this pandering deliberately ignores the clear, intricate artifice of rap braggadocio.

Yet there is something new in 'Hit 'Em Up' in terms of adding levels of vitriol and ingenuity to pop's proverbial 'answer' record. Tupac made the track to address his suspected attackers in the infamous 1994 ambush; he follows the same below-the-belt strategy Roxanne Shante used that year in her no-sisterhood throw down 'Big Mama.' Female rappers Isis, Salt'N Pepa, MC Lyte, Queen Latifah, Monie Love and YoYo, who Shante suspects stole her thunder, all get dissed in a mean but spirited fashion. ('Niggas came in flocks / For blocks and blocks and blocks / To watch the Rox / Knock the bitches out the box.') Shante's little-girl voice took infectious, juvenile glee in talking dirty. She flung shade through imaginative rhymes and jokey invective that Tupac in 'Hit 'Em Up' repeats but with a very male substitution of physical violence for metaphorical devastation.

As rap rivalry goes, 'Hit 'Em Up' is an inferior answer to The Notorious B.I.G.'s 'Who Shot Ya?,' itself a B-side riposte released after Tupac suggested Biggie Smalls and Sean 'Puffy' Combs were involved in his 1994 shooting. This battle of the MC's was as much macho animus as a contest of artistry. Although Tupac hurled a high level of cuss words and explicit intimidation, for anyone interested in the art of rap, the ball clearly remained in Biggie's corner.

Your Entertainment, My Reality

A master of the sly slaughter, Biggie showed how lyrical language can be made to thrill and kill: 'Fuck all that bicker and beef / I can hear sweat tricklin down your cheek.' Biggie, of course, wrote 'Warning,' one of the most audacious subtle lyrics in all of pop: 'There's gonna be a lot of slow singin' and flower bringin' / If my burglar alarm starts ringin'.' On 'Who Shot Ya?' Biggie had already announced 'I feel for you like Chaka Kahn / I'm the Don / Pussy when I want / Rolex on the arm / You'll die slow but calm / Recognize my face / So there won't be no mistake / So you'll know where to tell Jake / Lame Nigga / Brave Nigga / Turned Front-Page Nigga.' Aiming these sharpened thrusts, Biggie trumps like a cultural impresario, conjoining Chaka Khan's Black pop totem to his sarcasm, while his backing vocalists ruthlessly mock Tupac's five bullet wounds ('We proceed to give you what you need').

The only Tupac lyric Gilmore quotes – and at length – is 'Hit 'Em Up''s vituperation: 'You want to fuck with us, you little young-ass motherfuckers? . . . You better back the fuck up or you get smacked the fuck up . . . We ain't singin' we bringin' drama . . . We gonna kill all motherfuckers. Fuck Biggie, fuck Bad Boy . . . And if you want to be down with Bad Boy, then fuck you, too . . . Die slow, motherfucker.'

To this Gilmore exclaims:

I have never heard anything remotely like Tupac Shakur's breathless performance on this track in all my years of listening to pop music. [He must have missed Chuck D's 'Live and Undrugged' and Johnny Rotten's 'No Feelings.'] It contains a truly remarkable amount of rage and aggression – enough to make anything in punk seem flaccid by comparison. Indeed 'Hit 'Em Up' crosses the line from art and metaphor to real-life jeopardy. On one level, you might think Shakur was telling his enemies: We will kill you competitively, commercially. But listen to the stunning last 30 seconds of the track. It's as if Shakur were saying, 'Here I am – your enemy and your target. Come and get me, or watch me get you first.'

The brother of serial killer Gary Gilmore should know better than to take such trash talk to heart and then risk the libel of implicating both Biggie and Bad Boy Productions in Tupac's murder – except that the mainstream media liberally besmirches the activities of young Black males. Gilmore doesn't explain the intensified rivalries of East Coast–West Coast hiphop factions that turned teenage tribal spats into entertainment, a bad corporate joke on the smaller stakes of real-life street gangs. Such writing only feeds lurid, racist suspicions. But *Rolling Stone* doesn't care about Black artistry. The blunt, unimaginative threats of 'Hit 'Em Up' stand out to conventional music editors like a street mugging – perfect opportunity to editorialize.

Geeked up on Black 'rage and aggression,' Gilmore wasn't listening very closely to 'Hit 'Em Up.' He missed the track's circular background mantra – 'Get money!' – that exposed Tupac's intention to hew closely to the line of caustic but lucrative performance – the guiding aesthetic principle of gangsta rap. (Junior Mafia's 'Get Money' is one of the signature hiphop releases of the age – Barrett Strong's bastard child.) These showbiz/reel-life challenges, dramatized on disc, waste the youthful ingenuity that hiphop at one time applied to African American history and political strife. Now it's used (and validated in the mainstream press) to exaggerate dancefloor/Jeep competitions. That's still where the battle is won.

Despite this rivalry, brotherhood was displayed when it counted – on *One Million Strong*, the Million Man March tribute album, Tupac and Biggie are united for a cause. Their track, 'Runnin',' resolves all petty feuds, giving hope to the possibility for rappers to come to their senses, to understand that unity in the face of Black social need is more important than industry-sponsored pissing contests.

'Runnin'' survives from an earlier period – August 1994 – before bad blood flowed between Tupac and Biggie. Tupac issued an official 'no comment' about the song's inclusion on

Your Entertainment, My Reality

One Million Strong, but Biggie put the ironic track into focus when he told a reporter, 'I support any brother who wants to move in the direction of more responsibility to our unity. We're all trying to get paid. Anything else is just bullshit.' The terms of Tupac's rivalry with Bad Boy Entertainment coarsened what had been a healthy competition in hiphop.

Of the many essays written after Tupac's death, most are like coatracks the writers use on which to hang their favorite theories. Two exceptions: Darryl James in *Rap Sheet* and Harry Allen, writing in *Rap Pages*, brought the most knowledge and sensitivity to the subject without breaking down into maudlin excuses or valedictions. James provides an analogy to Marvin Gaye's 'divided soul,' based on the generosity of sentiment fans displayed, calling local Los Angeles radio station 92.3 The Beat, which set up a hotline to 'handle the calls of fans who did not know who to talk to or what to do, but found it difficult to process the death.' The Gaye comparison fits with the communal sympathy in Reverend Daughtry's eulogy that expressed Black American religious thinking (Daughtry's Jonah and the Whale parable fit popular notions of the rapper and the music biz behemoth with a moral perspective).

Allen's emotional flow staunched rumors of Tupac's resurrection and brought in telling details of Tupac's guiltlessness – as when flubbed stage directions at the 1995 *Source* magazine awards show led to 'Pac and his crew bum-rushing A Tribe Called Quest's moment of glory.

In his passion for Tupac and the entire misread hiphop culture, Allen also gave hints of Tupac's emotional life: 'Like the love depicted in Shakespeare's *Romeo and Juliet*, the classic play he adored, he too was verboten, forbidden, and so pure and undiluted that the world itself could not stand him.' That's Allen grieving – overcome rather than overstanding. But the *Romeo and Juliet* comparison is acute, working as an indication of Tupac's exploitation. Stephanie James, a student with Tupac at the Baltimore School of the Arts, remembers him reading

Romeo and Juliet with Jada Pinkett and Tupac later enthusing about one of her speeches; 'O, I have bought the mansion of a love, / But not possess'd it, / and though I am sold, / Not yet enjoy'd.'

As a youngster those lines must have clicked with how Tupac felt believing in the Panther ideas he was taught but did not yet benefit from. (The verse also evokes the 'love' Suge Knight offered with Death Row, love that Tupac bought but never lived to enjoy.) The romanticism Shakespeare evoked for Tupac fit an optimism in hiphop that came to be at odds with the nineties.

Fifties pop culture showed a better understanding of youth's tragic impairment when three Broadway hands – Arthur Laurents, that Panther sympathizer Leonard Bernstein and Stephen Sondheim – updated Shakespeare's exploration of cultural antagonism in *West Side Story* to address American class issues – the ruin of love by poverty and racism. As Gregory Solman points out, Baz Luhrmann's degraded *Romeo and Juliet* avoids Shakespeare's point about a society that uses its children as chattel. This is the necessary truth virtually every Tupac memoriam has avoided. It requires too painful a look at how even loving fans and rich executives got high off Tupac's blood.

But mostly the post-mortems have continued the media assassination that hiphop has fended off from its beginning. And it still threatens to engulf Tupac's legacy in confusion.

The shameless dream hampton had at Tupac again in several obits, her infatuation turned necrophiliac. You wonder how the supposedly socially responsible media could conspire to have hiphop chronicled by writers so insensitive that they print, 'Having attended dozens of funerals for young Black men in the past ten years, most of us must admit a certain numbness to violent death.'

The after-death notice hampton did for *Rap Pages* begins, 'Because we are a generation that has made and lost millions in the billion-dollar crack industry . . .' She doesn't critique capitalism, it's her primary tenet; lost dollars mattering more than lost life. Venality registered, she continues, 'And while, like a lot of women across the country, I was reduced to heaving sobs for the loss of Tupac Amaru Shakur, what's settled in its place is the calm that comes when one has completed an incredibly suspenseful novel. A sigh of relief is breathed; finally the drama – the roller-coaster ride – is over.' This is so distant from the difficult facts of life, it's no wonder hiphop fans and artists who take such writing as a clue to how the culture can be experienced end up relying on fantasies, half-truths, nonsense and pseudo-politics.

Pearl Cleage repeatedly worries, 'I'm too old to be writing about Tupac Shakur. My daughter made me do it.' But what's worse is her ignorance about aspects of Black living that this event should have clarified. 'I grew up with the Civil Rights Movement, the Vietnam War, Women's Liberation. I know what struggle is and I accept the inevitability of conflict, but I don't understand what it feels like to risk your life walking down the streets of your own neighborhood. I don't know how it feels to live a statistic . . .' writes Cleage. This is no help; it could be the result of hiphop not breaking through to some intellectuals, but a writer should be able to recognize the pieces of experience that are left out of certain artistic scenarios. Boys who bluff 'Back up off me' are not rampaging egotists; life teaches you those bluffs are methods of staving of fear. In sentimentalizing Tupac's tragedy, writers neglect what they ought to know based on other art or their own lives. Cleage nostalgically recalls, 'One big difference is we knew who the enemy was,' implying the sixties sense of the government-as-enemy but forgetting the competitive nature of society that expects and condones cultural opposition – boys against boys, men against women, white against black, rich against poor.

The urban reality of anarchic violence isn't new. Without the basic sense of civility to notice everyday killing and brutality, all the 'Stop the Violence' pomposity will get nowhere. Cleage reverts to sentiment when she says, 'I am not in the habit of lusting after convicted sexual abusers just because they also happen to be charismatic musical geniuses. Miles Davis broke me of all that, but I never thought Miles could be saved. Tupac was different. He seemed to be crying for salvation, struggling for clarity, searching for sanity in a world clearly gone mad.' When Cleage separates Davis's sins from Tupac's, she fails a clear-headed analysis of the patriarchy that binds them.

Sanyika Shakur, writing from prison, brings intelligence to Tupac's legacy but can't resist the eulogist romanticism of saying, 'Tupac was a rider, a courageous young brother and a street soldier.' Sanyika then forgets to distinguish between those roles. It's as bad as R. J. Smith writing in *Spin* that Tupac 'went out like a champ.' But Sanyika knows better when he scrutinizes, 'In all honesty [Tupac] did tend to buzz about as if he alone were privy to some deep secret that would soon unveil itself. However, upon closer examination of his material and indeed his actions, it would appear that he was just in tune to the maniacal machinations of this menacing society.' This too may be an excuse, but at least it's an insightful one with the force of truth.

The legacy is more shoddily attended in the white press – even by Black writers. Veronica Chambers apes dream hampton's smitten monkeyshines; in a tearful Tupac Lives! wetdream, she meets Mr Makaveli in his hide-out in Cuba, every radical's tropical hang-out. This tabloid fever dream isn't the only bad taste *Esquire* shows. Ivan Solotaroff's report on Tupac's last night in Las Vegas indulges the same grisliness as *Spin* magazine when noting the Thug Life abdomen tattoo, then speculating how surgeons cut into it.

Even Chambers exploited Tupac as much as possible, supplying *Esquire* with this:

> Tupac had a hard time following rules. Half the time there were no problems at all, but it wasn't unusual for Tupac to

get high in his trailer, to be hours late to the [*Poetic Justice*] set in the morning, or to get pissed off for what seemed like no reason at all. Once, toward the end of the shoot, Tupac was told he could have a day off. That morning, the producers decided that they would shoot publicity stills and called Tupac to the set. He arrived with his homeboys and began screaming, 'I can't take this shit. Y'all treat a nigga like a slave.' He stormed off to his trailer and promptly punched in a window.

Chambers had made no effort to understand this behavior when she was writing the promotional 'making-of' book for *Poetic Justice*, but after Tupac's death, she lets the dirt fly. 'At the time,' she demurs, 'nobody knew how far he was willing to take his mantras about living a 'Thug Life.'' (Though Chambers never reminds *Esquire* how far Hollywood took its apprehension by forbidding John Singleton to cast Tupac in *Higher Learning*.) 'There was indignation on the set about being blasted by some young punk but there was also fear; fear both *of* Tupac and *for* Tupac. I believe this was a pattern of concern that those around him felt right up until his death.'

Most of the media's Tupac legacies amount to cruel dissections – but not helpful ones. The *New York Times* put stereotypical myth into the record. A front-page headline read: TUPAC SHAKUR, 25, RAP PERFORMER WHO PERSONIFIED VIOLENCE, DIES.

At least Tupac, as a money-making star, got more respectable treatment from the *Times* than did Huey P. Newton, who had the bad style to die the same day as Diana Vreeland (so *Vogue*'s trendsetter got front-page treatment while the leader of a Black American freedom movement was squeezed in on the back pages). Jon Pareles's front-page story blandly pronounced judgment as historical fact, calling Shakur 'a rapper and actor who built a career on controversy,' but that's from a disdainful point of view that ignores the charismatic emotional attraction that compelled listeners to actually buy records. There's more sense in his later paragraphs: 'In some raps Mr Shakur glamorized the life of the "player" ... he described gangsterism as a vicious cycle, a grimly inevitable response to racism, ghetto poverty and police brutality.' But the transformation of 'gangsta' into gangsterism slyly changes an ineffectual social aberration into a major crime.

Rap, more than any other cultural form, has exposed the condescension in journalism – nowhere more than in the *Village Voice*'s objectification of Black cultural stereotypes. The *Voice* made entertainment of Tupac's trials, running feverish speculations about his shooting and hospital release as the lead Music Section story (meanwhile neglecting to review the simultaneous release of Scarface's solo album *The Diary* – an extraordinary musical work that is the model for the psychological expression Tupac openly imitated). Tupac became a favored rapper for hip journalists because he exemplified white Negro fantasies more than other rappers – L. L. too sane, Chuck D too political, Speech too erudite, Geto Boys not slick enough, De La Soul too idiosyncratic.

In the *Voice*'s special obit section Tupac was deemed to be THUG FOR LIFE and a coterie of wannabes held forth with the adolescent claim: 'High school is such a fantasy world it provides the sole complete analogy to hiphop' – a way to infantilize Black artistry. For the *Voice* the ubiquitous black widow dream hampton blamed Tupac's death on Suge Knight, while cutting into that tattoo again. Nelson George belittled him as 'it,' calling Tupac a 'tan DeNiro.' Only Natasha Stovall managed some genuine reporting that included Rosie Perez's phone-call to Monie Love's radio show: 'Tupac was not a dark-sided man. He was a misguided man. And I think that we all have to take some responsibility for how he went down . . . I should have had more courage, been more patient with him, and said, "Listen you're not going to push me away, you're not going to go with these new friends. I'm going to keep telling you, No, I love you."'

Death doesn't change the mainstream press's attitude toward

hiphop; it's still viewed as a dangerous, alien form. *Rolling Stone* and *Spin*, the nation's largest circulated pop music magazines, regularly restrict hiphop acts from their covers. *Rolling Stone* posthumously lauded *All Eyez on Me* as 'one of rap's few full-length masterpieces,' then gave a severely biased, brief history of recent rap:

> Rap began to report on and reveal many social realities and attitudes that most other arts and media consistently ignored – that is, rap gave voice and presence to truths that almost no other form of art or reportage was willing to accommodate. Works like N.W.A.'s 'F – tha Police' and *Niggaz4Life* (Actual title: *Efil4zaggin*) may have seemed shocking to some observers, but N.W.A. didn't invent the resentment and abuse that they sang about. Nor did Ice-T, Ice Cube or the Geto Boys invent the ghetto-rooted gang warfare and drive-by shootings that they sometimes rapped about.

Left out of that synopsis is Public Enemy, a rap group very much involved with 'reporting' urban struggle and mayhem. Tupac made no secret of his love for PE's album *It Takes a Nation of Millions to Hold Us Back*, but PE's political explanations have always been disapproved of by the mainstream music press and so are left out of histories slanted toward a segregated view of American culture.

Absolution is the point of these articles – absolution for indifferent Americans but mostly for those who cosseted Tupac, plus writers and professionals in support of the most destructive industry practices. *Rolling Stone* suggests, 'Death Row and Bad Boy could have a true and positive impact on black America's political life,' assuming those companies and that life have nothing to do with white America. *Billboard* magazine editor Timothy White wrote a merciless editorial decrying Tupac and letting the biz off the hook.

In *Vibe* magazine absolution reached a particular low when Danyel Smith recalled cheering on Tupac's first taste of success, celebrating his new apartment, new couch, flatware and a 'cedar-colored' maid. Noticing guns on a glass-top coffee table, Smith acknowledges, 'The firearms sat like dried piles of shit – not stinking but still foul.' Yet as the party went on with Tupac literally acting out the gunplay scene from Scorsese's *Who's That Knocking at My Door?*, the *Vibe* editor and friends indulged his recklessness. And that's the role the media played in Tupac's death. Not stinking perhaps, but still foul.

Tupac and Tim Roth in 'Gridlock'd'

Chapter Eighteen

Keeping It Reel

Against the many negative images of Tupac, there are those he actually approved in numerous music videos. Stephanie James remembers watching video tapes of *Black Caesar* and *Superfly* with Tupac in Baltimore: '*Superfly* was funny but it didn't mean as much to him as *Black Caesar*, cuz that had a Black man thinking up ways to control his neighborhood and his destiny. Like in *Shaft*. Tupac liked those because the heroes took control.'

TV pundits Siskel & Ebert once registered surprise that rappers made such good actors, but role-playing is a large part of what any recording artist does. It's especially important to rap stars. Tupac, looking for more acceptance, delighted: 'Yeah, I like that people come to me and go "*you* did a good job," when all my career it's been you guys this or that. I love it that somebody came and say, "Tupac, you a great actor, you did a great part." So now I want to do that even more and do other parts and do better parts. I want to do *Terminator 2* roles, something different so people can really see the diversity, cuz even now people, I think some people goin', "Now wait a minute, that's just him being him. How hard is it to be crazy?" Now I want to do something, you know, sane. I want to be in love or something so that people can see the diversity of what I can do.'

His last two film productions were aimed in that direction In *Gang Related*, a courtroom drama by writer-director Jim Kouf, Tupac stars with James Belushi, Leila Rochon, and in small parts James Earl Jones and Dennis Quaid. Belushi and Tupac are partners, two corrupt homicide detectives, who get involved in shady stuff and chalk it up to gang-related activity – the usual formula. But *Gridlock'd*, Tupac's first independent film, is another story. Written and directed by the actor Vondie Curtis Hall, it is credibly based on Hall's real-life experience of trying to get help and find his way through the big-city bureaucracies of drug clinics and rehabs. As members of a spoken-word trio, Tupac (as Spoon), Tim Roth (as Stretch) and Thandie Newton (as Cookie) play Detroit junkies who make a desperate effort to go straight, all the while facing inevitable death with gallows humor. 'You ain't gonna die, it's just a flesh wound,' Tupac says to Roth after a shooting. The line has eerie echoes; it works as part of the story which doesn't trade on Tupac's real-life woes but paints a gritty portrait of urban reality, satirizing the simplistic political notion of dead-end society. In a bold move for a first-time Black filmmaker, Hall breaks with Hollywood fantasy conventions, chosing a documentary style that manages to avoid all the pitfalls of TV-series realism.

Roth's appearance brings to mind *Meantime*, the signal eighties BBC film about life on the dole that he made with English director Mike Leigh. Roth's impressive British technique meshes with Tupac's naturalism, making them a good team. He remembers their working relationship fondly: 'My mate-name for Tupac was "New Money," because he was the upstart, full of the esprit of being a big pop record star and he was certain to be a smashing film star. He used to call me "Free Shit" because of the extra perks he thought I got in my dressing room, trailer, what have you.' Together, they avoided the hooey-quotient of actors getting high on playing druggies.

Gridlock'd deftly shifts dramatic tone from slapstick comic (a welfare office riot) to horrific comic (a hospital waiting-room nightmare). Hall, who starred in the memorable eighties theater production *Williams & Walker* (about the moral crises felt by twenties blackface performers Bert Williams and George Walker), lets the actors explore the complexities of good luck and bad breaks. Remembering Tupac, he said: 'When you think about George Walker and Bert Williams, they were completely different individuals off the stage and 'Pac was a lot more stuff than he seemed when outside the rap arena. The producer Preston Holmes got him the script and he said, "I want to do this movie." The brother showed up, he had the script down, had the character's arc. He could talk about the beats, he could make reference to all the shit. I thought, "This is not the cat the media is throwin' out there." He's smart, funny, well read.

'That's what saddened me about his death, you could see the compassion *and* silliness. In the media all you see is the picture with the hat skewed to the side, not even the pictures of what he was looking like when we were working. Just a straight up Black man.

'I went to the memorial benefit his mother gave. Ex-Panther after ex-Panther spoke. When you talk to the folks 'Pac grew up around, you sensed why the brother was like that: sitting around with his mother's friends, having the revolutionary brothers have dialogue at table and sense his mother's spirit and brilliance. It was evident when he was on set. He could reference any shit – it was because he was around fuckin' intellectuals when he was born. [He had] a diverse taste in music. The guy pulls up the girl in The Cranberries. He knew every artist out there. All these films, all this music; he sort of absorbed all this stuff.

'One time when we were driving in LA in his Rolls-Royce Corniche, he had the Cranberries blaring. He was on Crenshaw Boulevard. Some brothers pulled up, said "'Pac, what you listening to?" "Just the radio," he said. But it was the CD.'

Hall appreciated Tupac's eclectic qualities. He knew that actors, like rappers, when intuitively in sync, reveal their poignant secrets. *Gridlock'd* marked the first time since *Juice* that Tupac had had worthy collaborators who understood his pressures. Hall envisioned a trenchant hope: 'Tupac's movie career could have brought out more sides of his personality, so that people could know him better.'

Tupac had always wanted to act out revolution in real life. Years earlier, explaining the meaning of THUG LIFE, his motto and tattoo, he talked of a plan to start a camp for children on the order of L. L. Cool J's but with a different, militant purpose: to teach kids how to use firearms. Tupac had launched into an energetic proselytizing, full of race-war threats and mounting panics that only made sense as an expression of his own churning anxieties As he spoke, and his fears uncoiled, he exuded more and more unreachable certainty.

It was this ambition and mood that inspired the movie-parody concept of the *California Love* video. Directed by Hype Williams, the hiphop video director specializing in Hollywood knock-offs, Tupac was cast as an apocalyptic scavenger, modeled on characters in *The Road Warrior*. *California Love* exhibits his firebrand mania in images already accepted in pop culture. Though its source is trivial, Tupac embraced its form to validate his personal longing for apocalyptic action. Williams hypes it up with overlapping images and sped-up chases, disco fantasias, fight scenes that have nothing to do with the song's lyrics – all of which totally contradict, and perhaps parody, his second, conventional video of the song set at a party in contemporary LA. These compacted hiphop visions convey how hard it has become for young folks to stabilize their passions, or choose sensible paths. They're overflowing with feelings – emotions that need to be sorted out, examined, balanced, corroborated.

Rap Sheet editor Darryl James, writing of meeting Tupac, observed, 'The Tupac who stood in front of me then was just a cool kid who was funny as hell and just wanted people to like him.' That's the Tupac immortalized in *I Ain't Mad at Cha*, a video he co-directed that imagines his death by gunfire and his ascension to heaven where he greets Black pop stars from Billie Holiday, Redd Foxx to Jimi Hendrix and Sammy Davis Jr. James remembers the hopeful young star who said 'I never had shit growing up, so I had nothing to lose. Now I want to show what I've been through to other people who've been through the same thing to show how narrowly I escaped. I stand up for something: I want to take the bad and turn it into good.'

I Ain't Mad at Cha dramatizes Tupac's bonding with his homey (played by Bokeem Woodbine), shifting back and forth between heaven and earth so Tupac can keep an eye on his friend's reactions and see him being inspired by Tupac's death to keep on keeping on. It recalls another unexpected favorite film of his, Steven Spielberg's *Always*, in that love is so strong it keeps going beyond the grave. Tupac's theatrical instincts were shrewdly apparent in *I Ain't Mad at Cha*. The caring expressed in the video and its link-up with the Black showbiz tradition are true to the kinds of sincerity and fraternity that hiphop revived for a new generation of Black pop fans.

Picking up on the song's message of forgiveness, Tupac's video dramatizes the particular confederacy between his spirit and those of legendary pop stars. Looking past the egotism of this mini-drama, it vividly depicts Tupac's desire to connect and identify with others who have left an 'immortal' mark on the world through their achievement in the performing arts. It's significant that his heaven is not filled with political dissidents and rebels; the stress of Death Row had taken him beyond those factional concerns.

Keeping It Reel

I Ain't Mad at Cha tells all those who had offered him political solutions that he has seen his own world and time in a different light. He has defined his personal struggle in new terms. In addition to being a Black American male – an endangered species – he is contending with the complications of being an entertainer, of standing with one foot in the system and one foot in the street, reaching for the very top. In the pursuit of artistic expression and a public career – in spite of compromises and obstacles – Tupac has found challenge and reward enough. The optimism of this video conveys Tupac's desire to transform his earthly struggle into a quest for enduring fame and lasting remembrance . . . for paradise and redemption.

Tupac rarely admitted this drive, preferring instead to speak through hiphop's usual bravado in which 'keeping it real' meant limiting himself to ghetto stereotypes – what video director Mark Romanek calls 'brick-wall videos' that present hiphop performances in typical, predictable slum settings. In *I Ain't Mad at Cha*, Tupac goes one step beyond cliché, daring to resist the 'street' trend for a music video vision that brings him closer to an epiphany – and closer to examining the hereafter alluded to in so many of his raps. Partly inspired by Bone Thugs-N-Hamony's *Tha Crossroads* video that spans the Black church to the afterlife, Tupac represented hiphop sentiments in a setting that might even have charmed Reverend Daughtry. Keeping it 'reel' in this case meant an unusual effort to keep hiphop spiritual.

Video-making fully utilized Tupac's rap and dramatic ambitions. Leila Steinberg testified to the hiphop faith he had shown in 1993 when Mac Mall, a struggling Bay area rapper, needed a video to promote his single, 'Ghetto Theme.' 'I played it for 'Pac,' Steinberg remembers, 'and he said, "I'm gonna be a director, so this is where I'm gonna start, with the video, I'm gonna direct, you gotta let me." Actually he didn't give us a choice.' The chance to make images that expressed his feelings for life in the hood inspired Tupac. 'I love the song,' he said. 'I feel it. This is my project.' Putting his seal on a ghetto anthem – even on someone else's – showed Tupac's awareness of the importance of confirming hiphop's complicated experience. 'Video's a signal,' he said. 'So you turn it up!'

I Ain't Mad at Cha envisions sorrow, remorse and forgiveness, as clear and concise as Tupac would ever manage. The video's wishfulness may seem naïve because of hokey directorial devices and low-budget scenery, but it suggests that, up to the time he adopted his *alter ego* Makaveli, Tupac sharpened his ambitions while he outraced his dreams.

Afterword

This is a sad story, but it fits in with the complexity of love that survives in Black pop. To make the most sense of Tupac's life, there is need to attach it to the efforts of contemporary Black artists who, similar to Tupac, struggle with the effort to achieve and survive. The fact that listeners love Tupac so much weighs immeasurably. And love may hide all faults, but criticism can't. Responding to Tupac's art fully, honestly, requires critical thinking because it's a response to a version of the world that one can either recognize or dismiss. It is, as a recent book of poems and essays about Tupac asserts, *Tough Love*.

Tupac's conflicts over morality, behavior and politics reflect a familiar Black American dilemma – conflicts no caring person can disavow. Rappers are no different from other working people who try to rationalize their subservience to a system that wears them down, but the history of Blacks in pop music is complicated by the phenomenon of a people uniting the stress of hard labor with the enjoyment of a past time. What worked in Tupac's favor is that the recognition of these conflicts stems from something very personal and also universal: the struggle for a decent living. It's as radical as it is simple. And so, in place of answers to Tupac's death, I have pursued musical clues to his life.

Thank God they echo throughout American pop cultural history, in the legacies I got from my parents, my brothers and my sisters and my friends. I remember my own youthful excitement about the opening of the 1964 New York World's Fair being dampened by TV news broadcasting a boycott of picket signs and protests from the.old Congress of Racial Equality. Why spoil a happy occasion? I asked my older brother. 'Because they have to,' he responded with an air of serious dedication. 'They have to take whatever opportunity they can to get people to know the importance of what they believe in.' Imperative has glowed for me ever since and it's not far-fetched to imagine that glow lighting up Tupac's face as he told his future to Reverend Daughtry. It's for the good taste and caring such mentors showed me that, when I think of Tupac, the best thought I can come up with is mixed with the complexities of trust, disappointment and love. Dialogue from Tupac's first acting experience, *A Raisin in the Sun*, sums it up – and it keeps my head ringing: 'You feelin' like you better than he is today? Yes? What you tell him a minute ago? That he wasn't a man? Yes? You give him up for me? You done wrote his epitaph too – like the rest of the world? Well, who give you the privilege? There is always *something* left to love.'

Caught between affection and dissatisfaction, Tupac's love songs are the clearest expression of hiphop's emotional morass. 'Dear Mama' and 'Papa'z Song' are, despite their bitterness, love songs – but the only kind of love song a tormented young adult can muster. The young person who rages at the world so single-mindedly also struggles to honor his perplexing foundations and the guardianship that brought him to such a precarious position. At heart, it's a generational rift between

Civil Rights era self-esteem and hiphop era issues of dignity and independence. Each generation's indebtedness to its forebears' way of thinking and doing is subtly queried or alluded to in every hiphop art work.

This includes William Gunn's great play *The Forbidden City*. Gunn, the filmmaker and actor, best known for his script for *The Landlord* and his psychological vampire movie *Ganja and Hess*, was not an artist of the hiphop generation but *The Forbidden City*'s première the day after his death in 1989 (the same year as De La Soul's *3 Feet High and Rising*) resembled a passing-of-the-torch in Gunn's complexly imagined summation of Black survivalist wordplay and mind games.

Gunn's heroine, Miss Molly, reacts to the racist world of the thirties with a hardened bravura that bewilders her husband and her one remaining son, Nick Jr. In a bizarre echo of Afeni's own dejection, Miss Molly says, 'Gumption seldom does colored men any good. It'll most likely get you killed.' She remembers an infant son's death by attrition (a killing that recalls Bessie Smith's) and raps a warning soliloquy to Nick Jr.:

> That year five thousand Negro men had been lynched in North Carolina alone. At dawn, if you were sent on errands you could find somebody's brother or daddy hanging in a tree. It was the men they wanted. Why? What have you done? Is it something I don't know about? Why do you die so much? They let David die because he was a boy. I know it. Because he was colored and because he was a boy. Why are they so afraid of you that they murder little boys? Why? I'm in a stew because you can't kill back. And it keeps me from lovin' you too much, in case they murder the both of you.

The speech churns with much of the same agony that animates hardcore hiphop. Miss Molly 'brings the pain' (to use Wu Tang's phrase) – a personal assessment of race horror from slavery to the Atlanta child murders to contemporary police brutality. Gunn's tangled attempt to explore the consciousness of this legacy also shows up in Tupac's conflicted art – his ambivalence about his mother's failings and her own, undependable examples – on 'Part Time Mutha' he cites contradictory parental behavior and advice. Gunn's connection to Tupac can be seen in hiphop's basic contrary nature that starts from the current generation's response to the idea of domestic and social discipline.

So many of the most devastating lines in rap (such as Public Enemy's deliberately twisted anagram 'Ain't-how-that-God-planned-it?' from 'Fear of a Black Planet?') have to do with questioning authority and its lessons. Such challenges vibrate with youthful gusto, but that relish can leave a rapper confounded. Songs like 'Dear Mama' express a child's frustration with parental imperfection, thus (in Gunn's fevered drama) an impertinence toward history. Tupac's sea change of brotherly values in the irresistibly rabble-rousing 'Five Deadly Venoms' blocks the kind of commiseration with his forebears that can come with maturity, therapy or revelation. Ice-T made one of his best raps about 'The Hunted Child,' portraying the imperilled situation of young Black males dodging law and fate, but few rappers have honestly confronted hiphop's most characteristic figure: The Unhumbled Child.

Speculation on Tupac's distress assumes that he was on his way to enlightenment, close to a redemptive, loving vision of the whole world (the same wish favored about Malik Hajj El-Shabazz). But despite the fan's fantasies, there are no short cuts on the Road to Damascus and Tupac, apparently, was cut off before he got to his. Reverend Daughtry recalls the remove Tupac displayed when he said, 'I have to write what I know about, what I have lived, I don't know anything about the church or religion.' That was a part of his mother's discipline that the unhumbled child rejected. At the same time, it put distance between the rapper and that portion of Black compassion that is generated around the emotional warmth of the church – the public hearth in many working-class cultures.

You can hear this ardor on Blackstreet's album *Another Level*.

'Don't Leave Me' uses the same sample as 'I Ain't Mad at Cha,' the suave bragging of 'No Diggity' (a Number One hit) is matched by its opposite number, 'Motherlude.' In this production the four young singers end the album's quest for everyday meaning when they play back answering-machine messages from their mothers. Something of Afeni's concern comes through but it's stated from a fundamentally different principle than activism. There's obvious maternal adherence to Christian doctrine but what's extraordinary is the timbre of the women's voices. Each mother speaks in a personally derived version of church lingo ('God is able to do anything but fail. I'm prayin' for you and your group. Remember to put God first'). But the tone of voice is distinctively instructive ('I want you to think where God has brought you from; he has brought you a mighty long way'); patient ('I know one day you will be back home after you finish singin' this rock and roll'); kindly commending ('You been through a hard time strugglin' through your career but you kept pressin' on. You have been obedient, you have. Don't never forget where you came from and don't forget what your father has taught you. Always remember to do good, do right and be brave'); and devoted ('Teddy, you came a long way. You went the wrong way then God see fit to put in my heart to bring you back the right way, to tell you the right things to do. And so far you have prospered through your music and God have blessed you through song and music through your heart, through your fingers, through your mind').

They're all the mother's voice you carry in your head. To hear each woman respond to her son's success with the appropriate measure of gratitude and loving wariness is overwhelming. These taped messages are redolent of the life's work of child-rearing. Care and mercifulness are the ideas that come across, extending the feelings on 'Thank You for My Child' to the examples of how four sister souljahs deal with the awesome burdens of their children's success, fickle fortune, life itself.

Afterword

'Motherlude' precedes Blackstreet's own *pro forma* spiritual 'The Lord is Real (Time Will Reveal),' a Take 6-style haut-pop-gospel that manages to put forth the case of how a child is prepared for life by an elder's good example. These mothers have achieved their own transcendent social visions and are able to impart endurance and appreciation – not confusion.

The challenge to hiphop is to make the best use of the lessons history (and parents) hand down. Such a formidable task makes one react uncomfortably to Tupac's brash, ill-prepared rancor, because that unhumbled child had ingested a defeatist message that brought him up short. Tupac's pragmatism needs to be properly understood as just a part of the philosophical spectrum that hiphop can follow. In its simplified forgiveness, 'Dear Mama' reverses the benediction of 'Motherlude,' yet instead of revealing as much about what this generation of young men feel about life and obligation, it skips over the son's capacity for growth and faith. Not to blame Afeni's good efforts – a lesson taught also has to be learned – those gifts, plainly, were not imparted to Tupac and I want to present the side of the parent–child relationship that is possible in rap and is illustrated by still another poignant landmark of the hiphop era, R. Kelly's 'I Believe I Can Fly.'

Released after Tupac's death, 'I Believe I Can Fly' puts emotional heft behind the Michael Jordan-Bugs Bunny live-action-plus-animation movie *Space Jam*, a jolly, lightweight celebration of Jordan's ascendance to the mainstream. But Kelly, tasting his own burgeoning success, does something special with the concept. Like Bone Thugs-N-Harmony, whose second release tempered heady fame with metaphysical reflection in 'Tha Crossroads,' Kelly gets deep by getting spiritually high. Taking the next, necessary step after gangsta rap's nihilism, Kelly's romantic singing develops his New Jack smoothness into gospel, a remarkable new hybrid even better than Take 6 or such uplifting power pop as the Jennifer Rush/Celine Dion 'The Power of Love' or Gloria Estefan's 'If I Can Reach.'

Kelly's previous hit single, 'Down Low,' featured him in a quasi-Tupac role as a sneak-thief lover; in a remix rendition, he pulled out the stops for a breakthrough erotic groan. Yet the sensual extremes seemed more like a stunt than the natural fusing of sacred and profane ecstasy heard in Aretha Franklin's sixties classics. 'I Believe I Can Fly' takes Kelly there because the song's subjects – faith, possibility – directly relate to the hiphop era's concern with justice, Black potential, salvation over survival. Kelly's tremulous moans aren't merely orgasmic, but orgasm's correlative – the sound of a divine struggle. When he sings, 'I believe I can soar,' the aural play on 'sore' takes you back to the primacy of old Negro spirituals with their heaven and earth, pain and redemption multiple meanings. Kelly sets off a dynamic of moral sensitivities, the virtues instilled when a parent conveys that one's word is one's essence or that the help one does for others ennobles oneself. It's not a reversion to old, it's hiphop reclaiming the sustenance Black folks used to get from gospel.

Tupac evaded the political, moral instruction that would have taught him to connect his suffering and struggle to a redemptive idea (in 'Only God Can Judge Me' he seems to be citing religiosity by rote). But that does not mean redemption is impossible to speak of in hiphop. Tupac's agony comes from the limits people placed on how he should think, restrictions eventually put on the hiphop form itself. By making rap solely a report from the streets, hiphop censors what there is of Black America's own (good) news. 'Heaven Ain't Hard to Find' attempts Agape yet prompts a secular refutation reminiscent of Ice Cube's skeptical 'When I Get to Heaven.' The song ends *All Eyez on Me* perhaps because it's what Tupac wanted to say at the time. But what he really wanted was to find significance in earthly pleasure, physical excitement, the cruel world met on crude terms.

Discography

Tupac Shakur was just beginning to forge a career. Even this short list of record releases – all made within a six-year period – is, for a hiphop artist, extensive and ambitious. Hollywood, of course, was late to catch up, so the six movies listed merely scratch the surface of Shakur's rising charisma.

Singles and Albums

'Same Song,' *This is an EP Release* (Digital Underground) – Tommy Boy 0964

Sons of the P (Digital Underground) – Tommy Boy 1045

The Body–Hat Syndrome (Digital Underground) – Tommy Boy 0964

2Pacalypse Now – Interscope 91767–4

'If My Homeys Call,' Bust It 2 – Priority Records 3933–99458–2

Strictly for My N.I.G.G.A.Z. – Interscope 92209–4

'I Get Around,' Maxi Single

'Keep Ya Head Up,' Maxi Single

'Papa'z Song,' Maxi Single

'Definition of a Thug Nigga,' *Poetic Justice* Soundtrack – Epic EK 57131

'I Get Around,' *Straight From Da Streets* – Priority Records 4992–53885–2

'I Get Around (Remix),' *MTV Party to Go* Volume 5 – Tommy Boy 1097s

Thug Life Volume 1 – Interscope 92360-2

'Cradle to the Grave,' Maxi Single

'Pour Out a Little Liquor,' *Above the Rim* Soundtrack

Me Against the World – Interscope 92399-2

'Dear Mama,' Maxi Single

'Dear Mama,' *MTV Party To Go* Volume 7 – Tommy Boy 1138

'So Many Tears,' Maxi Single

'Temptations,' Maxi Single

'My Block,' *The Show* Soundtrack – Def Jam 314 529 021-2

'Throw Your Hands Up,' *Pump Ya Fist, Hip Hop Music Inspired by the Black Panther* – Avatar 69712 4048-2

'High 'Til I Die,' *Sunset Park* Soundtrack – Flavor Unite/East West 61904-2

'Made Niggas,' *Supercop* Soundtrack – Interscope 90088

'Me Against the World,' *Bad Boys* Soundtrack – Work/Sony 67009

'Runnin',' *One Million Strong* – Mergela 72667

All Eyez on Me – Death Row/Interscope 314–524 204–2

'California Love,' Single

Discography

'How Do U Want It,' Maxi Single

'2 of Amerikkka's Most Wanted,' Single

'Hit 'Em Up'/'How Do U Want It?' – Death Row/Interscope 422–854 653–2

'Slipping into Darkness,' *Day of the Dead* (Funky Aztecs) – Raging Bull Records 2011

'California Love,' *DJ Red Alert Presents*

'California Love,' *MTV Party To Go* Volume 10 – Tommy Boy 1194

'So Many Tears,' *Hip Hop's Most Wanted*

The Don Killuminati The 7-Day Theory – The New and "Untouchable' Death Row Records/Interscope 90039

'Smile,' *The Untouchable* – Rap-A-Lot Records 7243 42799–2

'Wanted Dead or Alive,' 'Never Had a Friend Like Me,' 'Out the Moon (Boom . . . Boom . . . Boom),' *Gridlock'd* Soundtrack – Interscope 06949

Filmography

Juice Directed by Ernest Dickerson, script by Gerard Brown. Paramount Pictures 1990

Poetic Justice Directed by John Singleton, script by Singleton. Columbia Pictures 1993

Above the Rim Directed by Jeff Pollack, script by Pollack. New Line Pictures 1994

Gridlock'd Directed by Vondie Curtis Hall, script by Hall. Grammercy Pictures 1997

Bullet Directed by Julien Temple. Trimark Pictures 1997

Gang Related Directed by Jim Kouf, script by Kouf. Orion Pictures 1997

Index

Index

Index

Index

Index